REIKI HEALING FOR BEGINNERS

Increase Your Energy, Decrease Stress

And Improve Health

DANIEL W. ALCOTT

TABLE OF CONTENTS

INTRODUCTION

Reiki is a spiritual practice everybody can learn from a qualified teacher. Learning what is commonly referred to as Japanese Reiki is simple, but it requires time like most good things in life. It also needs the ability to acquire, based on your awareness. A person cannot receive more than the level he can reach, determined by the standard he resonates with. This may sound not very easy, but it's not with a Reiki Shihan.

Furthermore, Reiki is a powerful cure device that allows a practitioner to place his or her hands on the customer without really controlling the body. It makes Reiki an excellent healing method for people suffering from physical and emotional problems of all kinds. Most clinics now provide Reiki healing as a relief and quicker treatment for their patients.

Also, this offers specific methods for achieving and sustaining internal peace and happiness, power, and immune systems. Methods include techniques of mindfulness and imagination, reflection, and meaningful thinking.

Conclusively, Reiki also provides a potent cure for any emotional "baggage," whether it's sorrow, anger, sadness or fear by smoothly releasing such emotions, usually without major disaster or curves. Reiki operates through the very gentle liberation of suppressed feelings just by harmonizing the negative impact and allowing energy to be released or recycled by the body.

CHAPTER ONE

Reiki's True History

REIKI's background is an ancient Tibetan process of healing. (Ray-Key is a Japanese word meaning universal life energy) Dr. Mikao Usui discovered REIKI in the middle of the 19th century.

Dr. Usui was the president of Kyoto Christian University, Japan. His students one day explained to him that they had never learned of Jesus Christ's healing. They asked Dr. Usui if he could make this kind of healing for them. Unfortunately, Dr. Usui had no answers for his students, and he left the university as head and set out on a journey to find the answers.

He traveled to America to study and graduated from the University of Chicago in theology. Instead, he learned in the Chinese Sutra and Buddha's cure in Japan and then in Tibet, where he studied the Tibetan Lotus Sutra and Sanskrit (the ancient language of India). There he found the answers he needed, the answers to Christ's healing ways. He now wanted empowerment.

He went back to Japan to climb the Kuri Yama Holy Mountain to fast and meditate on the Sanskrit method for 21 days. He placed 21 stones in front of him and removed one stone every day he passed by. Dr. Usui read the sutras all his time on the hills, meditated, and sang. Dr. Usui did this for 21 days, but until the very last day, nothing happened. As the day began, although it was still quite dark, and with some speed, a bright light traveled towards him. As it approached, it grew larger and reached him in the middle of the front.

He saw many tiny bubbles of blue, lilac and all the rainbow colors. Dr. Usui assumed that he was dead as a great white light appeared before him, looking up, saw the renowned Sanskrit symbols glistening in GOLD in front of him, he said,' Yeah, I remember' This was the development of the REIKI Usui system.

The sun shined high in the sky as he came to reality; he was full of enthusiasm, full of life, power, and courage, and even if he fasted on the Holy Mountain for 21 days, he ran down the mountain. It's been the first success.

He stubbed his toe in his sprint down the mountain. He covered it with his hands, and the bleeding stopped in a few minutes. That was the second wondrous miracle.

Dr. Usui knocked his toe in his rush to get down the mountain. For a few moments, he wrapped his hands around his foot, bleeding, and pain both disappeared. It's the second wonder.

Because he didn't eat in 21 days, he was starving, met him on the roadside of an inn, and ordered an extensive Japanese breakfast. After fasting, the innkeeper advised him not to eat that large meal. Yet Dr. Usui had no trouble finishing the meal. It's been the fifth wonder.

The granddaughter of the innkeeper had been dealing with a toothache for a few days. Dr. Usui gently put his hands on his angry face and instantly started to feel better. She ran to Grandfather, saying he wasn't an ordinary monk. The fourth miracle of the day was this cure.

Dr. Usui came back to his Kyoto abbey to treat the people of the town of Beggar and slums. In his seven years at the shelter, he found that the same faces came back to him. He told them why they hadn't moved on and began a new life. People explained to him that it was better to continue begging because it was too difficult to work. It surprised Dr. Usui and realized that during the healing, he had forgotten something essential, to teach beggars gratitude Dr. Chikiro Hayashi, one of Dr. Usui's closest colleagues, became the 2nd REIKI Grand Master according to the tradition. Before 1940, he ran his private clinic in Tokyo. He would deal with severe and unusual cases. A lady called Hawayo Takata was born on the island of Hawaii in 1900. Her parents were Japanese and a citizen of the United States. REIKI is administered around the clock. With two young children, she was widowed. Her journey led her to REIKI in 1935. At the time, when an internal voice told her to seek healing in Japan, she suffered from a severe illness.

In Japan, Ms. Takata went to seek healing. She was lying on the operating table when a voice spoke to her and explained that the operation was not necessary. He asked the doctor about other treatment methods and told him to go to REIKI Clinic, Dr. Hayashi. Initially, REIKI was administered to Ms. Takata by two physicians every day, and she had returned to full health in a few months.

Hawayo Takata was Dr. Hayashi's student for a year and returned with her two daughters to Hawaii. Dr. Hayashi made her Master when he visited Hawaii in 1938, and in 1941 she succeeded him as Grand Master. She was working, recovering, and training the REIKI Masters. Hawayo Takata passed away on 11 December 1980, leaving 22 REIKI Masters throughout the USA and Canada.

REIKI Therapy A REIKI therapy is provided to a client fully clothed, on a baseboard, or a chair. The practitioner puts his hands over or on the client. Depending on the care required, treatment can last up to one hour or sometimes longer. In the West, the practitioner would use the traditional position of the hand and then handle the essential parts of the body.

The hands are positioned gently on or above the client's body, so there is no pressure on the skin, which is suitable for all ages. The energy flows to where it is most necessary (spiritually guided). The customer has a hot tingling sensation in the skin. REIKI is a calming and stimulating experience.

Every person can experience REIKI in different ways, though everyone feels the feeling of deep relaxation, a glowing radiance flowing through and around him or her. Many people can go to sleep, and others can have supernatural dreams and hallucinations. In the end, the person is not only relaxed but also has a positive and balanced perspective.

Reiki is an effective cure REIKI can help with several complaints. Some of these are pressure management, relief from pain, nausea, stomach distress, back issues, asthma, breathing problems, PMT, menstrual problems, sinus problems, depression, and much more.

In some cases, REIKI assisted with full healings that were confirmed for medical tests before and after Reiki treatments. Although some have witnessed miracles, however, they cannot be assured. The most significant insight was stress management, with some physical and psychological changes.

REIKI should never be used as a compliment and way to become and remain healthy instead of medical treatment.

Reiki deals for medical or psychological care at regular intervals. If you have a medical or psychological problem, in addition to receiving Reiki therapy, you should see a licensed health professional. Reiki energy operates in conjunction and increases outcomes with all other forms of treatment, including medications, procedures, psychological care, or any other type of holistic care.

Although Reiki's power, in essence, is religious, Reiki is not a religion. Practitioners are not required to change their religious or spiritual beliefs. We are free to believe what we want and are allowed to decide for themselves the essence of their ethical practices.

REIKI Healing Benefits

It creates deep relaxation and enable the body to alleviate tension and stress.

This accelerates the ability of the bodies to repair themselves.

This leads to better health.

Blood pressure drops.

Encourages the immune function.

It can help with serious (injury) and chronic conditions (asthma, eczema, nausea, etc.) and can help break down addictions.

It can help to make the pain more manageable.

It helps the body to get rid of toxins.

It can help reduce medication side effects and help the body heal following surgery and chemotherapy.

It can increase the energy level and slow the aging process.

This raises the body's vibrational frequency.

This leads to spiritual growth and psychological clarity.

And finally, It can remove energy blockages, control the energy flow of the endocrine system, which regulates and synchronizes the body.

Can Reiki Heal Depression's Root Cause?

Depression is a cognitive or mental illness, turning the emotional state into despair and gloom, influencing the physical function and social interactions of an individual. Different kinds of depression include acute anxiety syndrome, dysthymia, bipolar disorder, seasonal affective disorder, postpartum depression, premenstrual dysphoric disorder, and atypical depression.

After all the forms of depression are listed, medical research and studies were carried out to determine what causes depression. The drug company has a pet theory that the brain's serotonin deficiency is a cause of anxiety or a chemical imbalance in the brain in the more general/basic sense. This hypothesis is developed when depressed people find that they have less than one form of the neurotransmitter, i.e., serotonin and norepinephrine. This chemical imbalance is sadly more a symptom than a cause. To better appreciate this, a simple explanation is that these low serotonin levels arise from more negative thinking and rarely take part in behaviors that provide personal fulfillment or happiness. In this respect, no study confirms or confirms the exact or precise root of the depression.

Others see depression as a biological disorder, but neither is it a virus that can be acquired or transmitted by others. "Animal Givens" in the 2003 book edition by J. Grip & I. Tyrrell, it was frequently repeated and stressed that depression is neither a disease nor a chemical imbalance. They defined depression as the spontaneous reaction of a person to a specific emotional introspection. Without a clearly defined or simple diagnosis and comprehension of the causes of depression, people often adhere to the closest or nearest medical explanation. The latest statistics on depression are troubling and indicate that an estimated 70 million people suffer from their symptoms that include but are not limited to inutility. These and other symptoms lead to self-destruction, beginning with pessimism, lack of motivation, and no initiative. Because of these negativities, the body and mind often obtain and transmit negative energies. This scenario often results in sickness, cancer, and other medical conditions. Other consequences could be desperation, irrational, or thoughtless decisions and actions that the person later regrets.

As disturbing as it is, everyone must take care to lower the numbers and keep them from further rising them. While the solution varies for every poor person, the common goal is to reverse the disease and restore the healthy life we all deserve. Through their various causes, religious approaches help depressed people to get out of the situation and to live a healthy, happy, and full life.

Depression, as previously explained, is not a chemical imbalance. This is not a cause of depression, and it is just a symptom. Many people say this and claim it's all in the subconscious, or it's a state of mind. The adult in a country of depression has lost the link with what is all about heaven, joy, and understanding as part of the quality of life. Neither medicine or research can fix depression change and conquer because their attitude and behavior are at stake.

To see a more holistic view of depression, the following as factors or a part of the cause of depression should be considered:

I. Health Factors: Physical or medical factors may cause a person to take a different view of life or mental health in life. You begin to feel and think negative thoughts and finally stop trying to contact optimistic about your situation. Hormonal imbalance, an unhealthy diet, the weak nervous system can impede positive life expectancy.

II. External Factors: Social status, culture, system, trauma, or weather can cause depression. People get sad and depressed sometimes when it's cloudy or raining. There's only something that attracts melancholy in the cold.

III. Emotional or Psychological Factors: Errors that cannot be overcome are also causes of depression. When a person is prone to engage in remorse and mistakes, he or she is surrounded by negatives, has grudges, jealousy, and envy that is likely to be depressed.

According to an associate professor (Harold Koenig, MD) at the Duke University Medical Center the spiritual power and holistic curing play an essential part in helping patients cope with depression and cannot be ignored as a variable. Studies have shown that strategies that include spirituality or religion are a better outcome as recognized by the annual meeting of the American Psychiatric Association held last 2002.

That groundbreaking finding paved the way for a different view of spiritual support. One should then pay attention to the values and religious practices of a person to find a better solution or treatment for them. While spirituality is not the only solution to depression, it is a great help if it is not healed 100 percent, then it can at least be made and finally resolved. Here are some examples and ideas on how spirituality can lift a person from a depressive state of mind. To ascertain the real cause, one must focus on the issue and spend time on it. It may even take days, and taking note of thoughts and having someone who can help you find the root problem would be helpful.

The right cure for the correct problem-Once the root problem has been determined, the correct solution can be found. If your question is physical or healthy, you can go to the doctor to resolve the trouble or pain that triggers depression. Exercise, diet, or nervous system stimulation by meditation or daily prayer will enable you to provide the energy for a physically and mentally regenerating person who helps to resolve a weak body and depressed mind.

If the issue is physical, emotional, or psychological, unhealthy behaviors should be avoided. Try to live a simple, pure, and just life by associating or encircling the right group of people and friends who have the same beliefs, are spiritually inclined, and have a positive outlook in life. Other people will help you face your challenges and struggles so that you are free of the depression you have retained.

Conclusively, if we have active spiritual assistance, we can control our bodies and mind. We can always be positive if we believe in something bigger or more powerful than we can help us. Reiki healing can help a depressed person greatly. The energy healing Reiki offers is more than adequate to project and provide positive energies from a Reiki healer to a depressed person. Reiki healing provides an immaterial gift (peace of mind and soul) to anyone who accepts it, and therefore a more holistic view, and a different perspective is a knowledge.

The Benefits of Reiki Are Healing Rather Than Masking

The next time you get to the bottle of pills, it allows me to heal, to mask, or to remove the effects of what needs to be treated. Such debilitating signs will continually reappear until an infection is cured.

The Mikao Usui power, called Reiki Ryoho, commonly known as Reiki, is at the root of what has to be treated and does not disguise the symptoms. Poisoning, as opposed to poisoning, is a natural process that often involves removing corporeal tissues or adding materials made by people to work with human tissues. As Reiki's benefits are recognized, the licensed medical practitioner, who not only has his or her health and education but the unique form of universal energy called Reiki that flows through him or her, is becoming less rare.

Reiki's spiritual practice balances the whole individual and is harmonious what is balanced and harmoniously healed. Reiki thus facilitates and accelerates healing deep within the mind, body, and spirit.

People today tend to miss this chapter, which explains why rest is the most important element of good health and how turning the motor Over prevents deflation and congestion. When there is little rest, Reiki focuses on maximizing the efficacy of food, medicine, and any therapy. Every tissue in your body has a specific function that ensures the maintenance of all processes. Growing tissue requires energy, and Reiki is an energy form that can respond to any necessary vibration. Many Reiki practitioners begin a session in a way that is most comfortable for them. The following are the tissues within the customer's body that guide the practitioner's hands and hold them in several places. Reiki flows to wherever there is a need, but the practitioners ' hands are directed to a certain place.

Many healing sessions take 45 to 90 minutes. Several imbalances in the body are managed more easily by several sessions. Kerry Bone and Simmon Mills Give a general thumb rule the time it takes to cure when writing about herbal medicine. I recommend three months of treatment for a disease of one year's standing and one month every additional year. Regular Reiki sessions are best received, but every person who works with a practitioner should work with what suits their life. Reiki will flow only as much as cells can hold. Once the energy is exhausted, it is best for the cells to receive more energy for repair, removal, and reconstruction. If you think of cells using fuel, go back to the ATP molecules that biology 101 has talked about. If there are no energy-needing imbalances, Reiki will flow to the whole person to boost repair, release, and reconstruction at every level in us. Many diseases come from failure to cope with infections that are not adequately defended in the body or body. On those days, when you have simply given yourself everything to a task, it is nice to feel that you are all recharging the peaceful way of a Reiki. Sometimes, after a session, people feel light as unnecessary pressures have been released with no pain or effort.

Many people doubt how a Reiki session can be cured if Reiki practitioners do not adapt, using needles, tuning forks, or something like that. The power of energy coming from the universe needs only the person through whom it flows to have learned the necessary discipline and to have achieved spiritual growth in order to open up to it. Today there are many trained Reiki Shihans (teachers), and it's easy to show them or their qualifications by testing a Reiki Lineage back to Mikao Usui.

If you have persuaded yourself that you can't cure or just ruin your life, your body follows the waves of emotion that you are drawn by such thought. Love and love are created in a calming and enjoyable Reiki healing session. In this safe state of relaxation, your brain waves slow down, and your thoughts drift away from the negative so that the positive can move in. With positive energy flowing into you, you feel that homeostasis takes place in your mind, body, and spirit.

When you put something you think you should do away with, you can see it in a different light. Headaches of tension become history. Chronic pain breaks give you the time to relax, to experience relaxation, and to gather your thoughts during your healing process. Pain drains a lot of energy, and relaxation and the unique energy of Reiki are important ingredients in the health and happiness recipe.

Reiki practitioners and instructors don't offer immediate remedies, but healing is performed in the manner best suited to every person who receives it. Reiki allows the whole person (or the individual as Reiki serves all of life) to rearrange their mind, body, and body, in a balanced way, after a wound, an operation, or other professional medical treatments. Through conventional medical procedures, the cartesian division of the body and mind can be reversed by Reiki. Reiki promotes drugs and therapies provided by medical professionals and helps prevent side effects.

Nobody knows better the body than you do. How many times did you know that something was wrong despite the negative medical tests? There are no tests with Reiki and, unless he or she is also a licensed medical professional, neither doctors nor teachers diagnose or prescribe therapies. Because Reiki travels to areas where no illness is present, cures may start early before a disease falls into the category of crisis. The more balance your mind and body are, the easier it is for you to heal from any sudden or accidental health crisis.

Reiki enhances the awareness of a person in areas such as vision, sound, smell, and taste. As Reiki goes to the core and shines from within like a flashlight, healing can continue two or three days after A session of healing. Chronic pain breaks that last for two to three days after treatment allow time for your recovery, your relaxation, and thoughts to be collected while you feel the healing. I had medical doctors inform me that in many cases, Reiki was incorporated; they never expected the healing to happen as quickly.

Reiki is often all the positive energy you need to feel right with the world again. Too often have you felt troubled by the dispute you had with your mother, brother(s), sister(s), a friend(s), teacher(s), child(s), girlfriend, landlord, or boss? Reiki can help a person develop more positive relationships. Reiki will flow to the workplace and make working days more comfortable by helping to remove obstacles and establish more positive relationships. One of the aspects felt after a Reiki session is cognitive calm. Although a person most often finds him or herself more comfortable, they are, after the session, energy-rich and ready to take on life.

Reiki will allow a new mother to return quicker with a zest for life and experience a relaxing feeling. It is what can be considered a "two-for-one deal" to obtain Reiki during childbirth as if it goes to the mother and the baby.

Many people have heard of SomatoEmotional and Cranial Sacral Therapy. Both treatments are performed by licensed physicians. Reiki gently helps the cranial cavity to flow, feels wonderful, and represents the equilibrium of these therapies without the risks of the parasympathetic nerves.

Reiki practitioners and teachers are wonderful listeners, but why you come to Reiki is not to be explained. Lesions and disorders can be extremely personal and, since the practitioner has learned to feel the inharmonious vibrations, his or her hands are instinctively directed in places that can use the most energy.

We hear today about many different Reiki forms. The religious practice of Reiki has been modified after Mikao Usui passed away in 1926 by many Reiki teachers. Every time a Reiki teacher changes the way it is taught, the name is changed to prevent the teacher from being dishonored. Sacred energy and divine energy are considered universal power. I refer to Reiki as the vibrations of the love and the harmony of universal energy described by my Japanese teachers Gendai Reiki-ho and Komyo Reiki. The words used don't matter, because the roots of the Mikao Usui method are deeply rooted in time.

When you study different Reiki types, before you develop that particular style, you can see the direction of the Reiki instructor and gain a better understanding of the different styles. Universal energy can never be changed, and so no Reiki style is better than any Reiki style session with nothing added, and the only demand of the customer is to relax and enjoy. The unique form of energy that flows through a trained Reiki practitioner is never harmful or has negative side effects.

The Ghostly Power of Change

There have been many publications about why we change, why we change, when we change, how we change, and who we can't change.

Some of the most common visible changes are physical appearance, dietary changes, habits, changes in residence, and job/career changes. Look closely at these changes and see the changes that have occurred to create these changes.

Changing your clothes is more than changing your appearance. The clothes you choose from your wardrobe rely on how you feel at the day and where you expect to go. The experience defines how you consider such items as clothes or shoes in your drawers or closets. Like your reality, this letter e makes a difference in the way you see these woven threads. Change your reality and what you wear can change.

There is a shift behind every visible change that triggered this transition, sometimes so invisible that you might not be aware of it. These transparent issues can sometimes profoundly affect our lives. The wispy image of a person whose body has stopped working is usually marked with a ghost. Plots based on those wispy energy sources that persist after the body is dead have led books to ascend to the best-selling list and box office films to crash.

Ghosts appear differently in the reality of each person, but they are all-powerful. The power to make some people laugh, to let some people freeze in terror, to make some people happy in good memories, to make some people run excitedly to get their phone, and to overwhelm others with sorrow.

If there are a dozen photos of an old hotel, they might be interesting. On the other hand, if a wispy image is present in one of these images, marked as a ghost, it is a magnet for most people's interest.

That's a lot of power for something that's switched from tangible to fuel, which isn't even able to heat your room. You may or may not know that every kanji in Japanese is translated in various ways. One of the two Japanese kanji translations for the word Reiki is a demon. This translation fits beautifully with the incredible force of transformation that comes about when the universal waves of unconditional love and peace are incorporated into the heart, body, and mind.

Thoughts such as Ghosts can seldom be seen but strong. Consider your last thought of changing from your formal wear into a pair of jeans. You may not have had formal wear or a pair of jeans although you had both the cash and the chance to buy them. If this is the case, why did you think stopped buying them?

Speak of your thoughts as threads. How you weave your thoughts into a faith will make a big difference in how you and your life see yourself. The book "Think and grow rich" has become popular in this century. Each language has rules of syntax; would it have the same appeal if the name of this book were changed to' grow rich and think?'

Those tiny threads that are just ghostly images have more power than we often acknowledge. In 1922, Mikao Usui said that his religious practice was focused on the path to health and happiness. In a simple translation, the Reiki Gokai (5 precepts/5 principles) reads in your mind as song morning and evening. Conversely, it can also be translated more accurately into your heart as singing; we use your mind to remember and figure, and our heart is where true knowledge takes place. A shift in words will make a complete difference in the way we interpret a thought.

Things and expressions can be undeniable, but the negative can also be the way we hear or see. Starting with the Usui Reiki Gokai, most Usui Reiki type techniques are structured to let the negative go and make the way we think is turned into the positive. Reiki isn't psychological stimulation, and it's just a spiritual practice that can relieve the negative. Once the negative is released, positive universal energy will flow to tens of thousands of cells to bring balance and harmony.

The shadows caused by trees in the vicinity of a garden can prevent plants from flowering. Switch the plant place to a sunny area, and it flourishes beautifully. Negative thoughts may also produce shadows, but wispy visions of the positive may shift the experiences within those perceptions when the darkness is removed.

The refusal of Rosa Parks to give up her bus seat in 1955 gave ghostly power to change for a long time. When arrested, she had no idea of the beneficial effect it would have on the movement for civil rights. Because of her own faith, Rosa stood on her ground. Beliefs that have been nurtured by positive events in our lives will help us move on so that our progress book is an ongoing project.

Nevertheless, values nourished by the negative will undermine our attempts in different areas of our lives. Tragedies that are sometimes not let go and constantly revisited will snowball into the nightmares of our everyday lives.

Imagine waking up in a nightmare, and the negativity left behind can be swept off, linked to universal, unconditional love and harmony, and then into a quiet space within your minds. Consider doing the same thing before you sleep at the end of your day so you can sleep peacefully. These are some of the exercises of Reiki styles that praise Usui Reiki Ryoho.

Within any Usui Reiki style, there is a ghostly power of change based on a spiritual practice that Mikao Usui created in the early twenties. You start to find the core (constant power) of universal, unconditional love and peace expressed in your Ki / Qi / Prana/life force when you begin to practice a type of Usui Reiki.

If natural or scientific healing is used, the final result of the healing lies with the patient and not with the healer. The cells can introduce new information/energy, but cells also have memories. Memories are yesterday's vague images that we can let go, learn from, or hang on to. Such subtle images can form assumptions that spur the tens of thousands of cells into positive or negative action in any life form.

Through experience, a magnificent warning system is established for your survival, but if a false cause is linked to the physical or mental pain you have had, you could block a road to something positive. If negative or positive occurs, a slight picture may add an individual, material object, smell, sound, etc. Once this connection to the subtle image of an occurrence is made, the catalyst for positive or negative emotions is placed inside you.

One way to lower the harmful faint images in your cells is to deprogram. You may link deprogramming with societies and conflicts, but it is more commonly used to clean the brain regularly unconsciously every day. Reiki types like Gendai and Komyo Reiki have a gentle yet powerful programming technique.

Reiki, Nentatsu, Hatsurei-ho, and Seihiki chiro-ho are methods that expel the negative and replace the positive ones you need in your life. In this century, a qualified Reiki Shihan (teacher) can easily be found that can help you release the negative and get you into the positive light best for you. The release and getting in promotes balance and harmony, which is what Usui Reiki's spiritual practice is all about.

CHAPTER TWO

The Strength of Reiki

Most people are in circumstances that they think someone else has made. The strength of Reiki when coping with helplessness You look outside of yourself for the trigger. We say, "I can't help" or "I just happened to be raped." Or, "I am here in this rented home, I have no income, I live on unemployment benefit. Somebody else decided I am handicapped, and I cannot work." In their eyes, others are always to be blamed. We often don't know they think like that.

Not everyone feels helpless, but in some cases, everyone has felt hopelessness. You have no responsibility for your own life in the early years, your family, or even foster parents. You want to break through this powerlessness during puberty, but other people pull you in line. This will continue if the acts towards maturity are ignored. Growing up ensures that these bonds are loosened and fully autonomous.

Why do people get stuck in this impotence?

It's something they care about. The notion of complete autonomy can be terrible. The territory is uncertain. If you are alone, you can't spot anybody else's repercussions. You can't hold another person responsible. You are fully accountable, so you need to know the strategies. People like to take the responsibility away from themselves because it's comfortable; that's how they grew up. Many people tend to be followers, and others are challenging. Rebels are often likely to overdo it. Such people have not grown up, so they blame everyone else and can continue to firebombs for their helplessness. Followers have even more trouble braking impotence when they become adults. To be a follower is as unbalanced as a leader. Our mother and father didn't give us any real examples of how to live separately. Independence gives direction, compassion, and social network. When you are helpless, you don't take the reins of life, but give them away.

Are there any steps to do this?

Yes, you can do things. The first step is to take responsibility as a child for your years. Whether you've been exploited or misused or something much less severe–you might not be able to go out or always wear a robe when you'd like to wear your jeans, or maybe your mother will cut off your hair and don't have the permission to go to the hairdresser. It can be anyway. The conduct is to be held accountable. "Here and now, you decide that you won't fall back on things like this," the doctor said so... My mom did this... That's what my dad said. "If you were maltreated and turned out to be autonomous, it means that you can say' I disapprove of this behavior.' While patterns are often repeated, you decide that you will never replicate a design from now on. When you become autonomous, you start to handle your old traumas and stop building new ones.

Systems of Chakra and Balance

It is widely accepted that the body's energy centers have an essential influence on the physical body, emotions, and spirituality. Most healing systems work to align different emotional processes in us, and many of the energy centers and roles also overlap. Nevertheless, the chakra method is an exciting concept, and its simplicity brings it to anyone interested in achieving well-being conditions. See below for essential clearing and energizing ways of the chakras.

Sanskrit word "wheel" is used to describe the centers of spinning energy in the body that holds the life force (chi) and affect the well-being of a person. It is suspected that they affect the glandular systems. The human body has a total of 15 main chakras, although the seven main chakras are the most well-known. There are approximately one hundred other small chakras. The color, sound, and light are correlated with each of these energy centers.

It is widely believed that the origins of the chakra scheme, as we know it, lie in the Vedic traditions of India; in two Hindu books, the Sat-Cakra-Niripama and the Padaka-Pancake, by the pen name of Arthur Avalon, published by Sir John Woodroffe.

Here are the characteristics of the critical system's seven most well-known and often handled chakras.

1st or Base Chakra (the energy of the life force of Kundalini, considered to be house and related to survival, money, and security) focuses on the base of the spine. The color red, the musical C note and sound "oh" (rhymes of "go") is associated with the **Second or sacral chakra** (which is linked to body problems and sexuality) placed in the center around the diagram area between the navel and the zone where the hips meet the spine. It is related to red, musical, D-note, and sound "OOO" ("you" rhymes).

The Third or Solar Plexus Chakra is located at the level of the navel, just behind it, associated with the will and personal power. It is linked to the color-yellow, the music note E, and the sound "ah" (the rhymes with "ha")

4th or love-associated Heart-Chakra in the middle of the chest at the heart level. It is usually associated with green color, but pink in some cases. It vibrates with the musical note F and the sound "ay."

The 5th or Throat Chakra is situated in the middle of the neck at the bottom of the voice box. It is synonymous with light blue tones, the music G, and the "eye" tone (as is the case with the letter "E").

The 6th or Third Eye Chakra is between the eyes, just above the forehead, correlated with insight and mental ability. The color Indigo, the musical note A and the sound' om' are related to this (rhymes with' home,' the mmm sign is the longest).

In the middle, just at or just above the top of the head, is the **7th or Crown Chakra** (connected with spirituality). It is related to the violet color, to the B musical note, and to the "nngggg" sound (rhymes with "singing"). Most exercises are performed to strengthen the chakras and reinforce them. Here's one that's pretty easy and funny.

Balancing the chakras with sound and color This is a fun exercise that takes only about 20 minutes. This combines the seven specific chakras effectively with the colors and tones that suit them.

If you want to practice away from your computer, print this page out as your guide.

Check for colored paper, gemstones, or objects in each of the above-listed chakra colors.

Sit in a comfortable position, take a few deep breaths, and get rid of the day's concerns.

At this moment, be aware of your body. How does it feel, how does it feel?

Begin with the red element for the first chakra, and look at the color as you make the related tone, keep the notes, allow the vibrations to move through the body, or concentrate on the chakra. Try and hold the record one or two minutes, if it's tough, you can just repeat it for one or two minutes.

Follow this process until you complete the crown chakra on each of the colored objects.

Pronunciation of the sounds:

1-"oh "Go

2-"ooo" You

3-" ah "ha

4-"-"ay" hey

6-"eee "bee

6-"om" home

7-"nggg" sing. As you get done, take a moment to get your senses back into your entire body. It's normal to feel a little lightheaded. Compared to the time you started; how do you think now? You will feel bright and clean.

The Chakras Spiritual Development

The creative life force sleeps inside each of us as a bobbed snake, waiting to grow humanity to the next level. Ancient Tantric practices awaken this power, kundalini, with body, breath, sound, and vision to speed up his voyage to the realization of God.

Man has three bodies: physical and conscious; astral or subtle, experienced as sensations and emotions; and causal as intelligence and wisdom. The seven chakras serve as transformers of energy for the three corps/minds that govern different functions. When each chakra is triggered, the body/mental is cleansed, matter spiritualized, and the consciousness increased. Gradually, energy moves on the seventh chakra from darkness, the negative pole, to light, the positives pole, and full awareness. The method was associated with western psychoanalysis.

THE FIRST CHAKRA: Muladhara is a negative pole in the coccyx. You are married to establishment principles at this stage. Security and independence are primary topics. Primitive energies such as fear, combat, and flight are common responses to physical or psychological attacks or injuries. You have extreme global fear that causes extinction. This chakra is related to anxiety, dependence, and severe dysfunction that can contribute to violence against others. These worries are latent in the average person, but may still affect your life. Where these desires are dismissed, they are interpreted as hurtful to others. Growth begins with the realization, integration, and transmutation of these fears. As subconscious thoughts or memories become conscious, more energy is placed at the fingertips for better functioning.

When the sleeping serpent awakens and rises slowly, you may feel the sensations of swelling, joy, and tingling and heat at the base of the spine. Vision or clairaudience may appear.

THE SECOND CHAKRA: The second, Svadhisthana, lies under the naval and over the genitals. Your senses and your nervous system become more sensitive to your physical and emotional effects. The emphasis is more on physical and sensual pleasures than on the safety of oneself. There is, therefore, more contact with others, even when they are sexual objects and a broader range of emotions, while subconscious desires and appetites still influence you. These procreative forces are powerful and can be physically and mentally extremely unpleasant unless articulated, sublimated, or guided upward. Meditation and tantric sexual practices provide for the canalization of kundalini to higher centers.

This chakra is the unconscious place, and once opened, you are filled with energetic, sometimes conflicting emotions. You show and follow all of your past circumstances and patterns, and, if not studied or worked through, the kundalini will descend. Higher transpersonal levels of consciousness can be reached only after you have successfully identified and incorporated your unconscious. There are warnings that unless you have enough ego strength, character, and faith in God, the unleashed energies can cause serious harm to the individual, from inappropriate romantic or sexual ties to mental collapse. In this chakra, awareness of the astral body and heightened perception are excited. Prophetic visions and accidental telepathic encounters can often take place.

THE THIRD CHAKRA: The Third, Manipura, is similar to the solar plexus. Control and power and the necessity to cater to your personal needs around the world are issues here. The goal is to ensure yourself effectively in the world without manipulating, dominating, or submitting yourself to others. Once Manipura wakes up, you become aware of your heart, gain control of your emotions, and thus begin to exercise power over your karma.

Many cultures find this to be the start of spiritual evolution because of the propensity for kundalini to decline if the difficulties of the second chakra were not endured. You can also have digestive problems here as the skin is cleansed. There are more ESP capabilities.

THE FOURTH CHAKRA: The fourth is between the breasts, the Anahata, or heart chakra. Once Anahata is entirely awoken, you are separated from your feelings. Feelings are less contaminated with addictions and needs. You know your thoughts and karmic patterns, but you can exercise free will to satisfy your wishes. Now the soul can guide your choices and actions more fully. With basic survival instincts and desires weakened (in the first three chakras), energy is free to concentrate on self-realization. This chakra is therefore called the crossroads between the earthly and the celestial, as well as the left (yin) and the right (yang). This is represented by the cross symbol and also by the six-pointed star composed of two triangles. Your mind is in the spiritual world, more and more.

In the heart area, you can experience stabbing pains. This is inevitably followed by a surrender of the fight for control and a willingness to become increasingly driven by the spirit. In the Jungian context, the ego and the self are more integrated and interrelated. As a consequence, there is less internal tension, more peace with yourself and with others, and less comparison and rivalry between good and evil. As you become more integrated and thorough, there is less effort and desire for others and more considerable attention, reactivity, and appreciation for others. You should give without obtaining or exploiting others for personal gratification. A positive approach to life emerges, which is considered crucial to sustaining the evolution of kundalini. Psychokinetic and healing forces appear, and the realization of synchronicity and wishes begins.

THE FIFTH CHAKRA: The fifth, Vishuddhi, is on his throat and thyroid gland. Third, CHAKRA Vishuddhi is associated with soulful imagination and language. It requires that the ego can be left aside and that higher self or creative intellect can be conveyed mentally and artistically. The throat chakra also controls the capacity of others to seek food and that of the divine. Gradually you gain a sense of confidence and security, realizing that limitless food comes from an inner transpersonal origin. Through engaging the unknown and respected spirit, you cultivate yourself in the creative act. You become more distant in the universe, more and more associated with the spiritual realm.

It is also said that this core controls our sense of time and space, whether we experience slowing or rapid motion, which influences the rhythm of our lives. Hearing can sharpen, and telepathic abilities can eventually develop.

THE SIXTH CHAKRA: The sixth, Ajna, is located near the pineal and hypophysial glands between the eyebrows. Sight and light are associated with the pineal gland. Once you trigger this chakra, you can see the light around the front. Intelligence and insight are improved. You should contact your superior wisdom or mentor. The inner vision obtained brings you beyond the physical and time, space, and causality limitations. You feel connected to nature and the entire universe. This wisdom represents a union of two kinds of intellectual and sentimental knowledge. The two nadis left and right, feminine and masculine, or streams, enter the caduceus Ajna chakra.

THE SEVENTH CHAKRA: The seventh, Sahasrara, is the positive pole at the top of the head. When this chakra is activated, the Door of Brahman enters open and divine energy symbolized by the crown, halo, or light. First, you have headaches and short moments of samadhi; all the other chakras are activated. Duration and effects increase with practice. Duality stops when fully engaged, and you enter cosmic consciousness, samadhi, or illumination. There are no more prolonged subconscious emotions or thoughts, or a division of self and the awareness of thinking or feeling. God is perceived as a state of being; You become pure consciousness, happiness, and you have a deep understanding of yourself and the true nature of everything and all dimensions.

Sahasrara is at the soft spot, which closes up gradually after the spirit comes into birth and opens up again to exit at death. Adepts will prepare for their time of death if their consciousness ultimately leaves their body. Orthodox Jews are wearing a skull cap to cover this area, while some monks are shaving to leave the field uncovered.

There are many ways the chakras are awakened. A summary of the Tantric yoga practices is given in Hiroshi Motoyama's Theories of the Chakras. One strategy is to focus on each chakra when gazing up the nose. The associated color on each chakra is also visualized, and the corresponding mantra is sung.

The order in which the chakras awaken differs from the karma and existence of each person. Most suffer from this powerful force physically and mentally, they cannot live a normal life, and they never enjoy the benefits expected. That is why it is important to study with experienced tutors and not to hasten the cycle.

The Power Of Reiki Symbols

There are many different types of healers in the world today, from auric healers to clear vision or psychics that we already have, and very few have records of Reiki Masters. Reiki originated in Japan around 1922, a type of healing hand that is known as an alternative form of medicine. Just as acupuncture appears to work with energy which passes through our bodies, Reiki is a healing practice that also forms our bodies ' energy systems, while transmitting fundamental energy through our eyes. This chapter will teach you about Reiki symbols and why they are so important today to inspire Reiki masters.

Reiki was invented by the Japanese Buddhist Mikao Usui, who was a very skilled healer. Although this medicine is known to be oriental, any person who is attenuated with the symbols by a Reiki master can use the same power to heal. Knowing that healing requires entering a state of perfect balance, the energy from your hands simply returns balance to a human. Because energy and matter are intricately related, as shown by science, by manipulating the flow of energy within humans, you can also cause physical change.

Two types of Reiki, In addition, there are two styles of Reiki widely used. One is known as the Japanese Reiki. The other is known as Eastern Reiki. The main difference is that conventional Reiki is more intuitive, in which the practitioner puts his hands in positions where he feels the power will flow. Western Reiki relies on a very systematic way to put your hands on the body of a person to make a switch. These both have three distinct levels, including the first level, the second level, and what is known as the master level. You will obtain the attenuation of all three grades only from a master teacher, and thus become a Reiki Master for yourself.

How Reiki works The reason Reiki can help people heal is that it can tap into what is called Ki. This is also called Chi in China, and in the culture around the world, it has many other names. Essentially, you tap the essence of the world, the energy from which everything came. Therefore, you should detach yourself from the situation and allow your inner dialog or perception of the world to pause for as long as possible so that the energy flows through you. You can access the healing energy of the world, and the signs of Reiki can help you do this. When a Reiki Master uses the symbols on all three stages, you'll have a greater chance of becoming a more professional healer.

Does Reiki work for all?

It is both yes and no that addresses this question. This works for everyone, but it may not work, depending on the situation. If a person is not cured by a Reiki Master or someone who has strength, healing could not be achieved due to both the healer and the person's strong frequencies. It is also important to recognize that the universe works on its own terms, and when the time comes, it is your time to go. We can only try our best to give people the best opportunity to recover from their disease or injuries, but Reiki does not work when what you are trying to do fails. Just as doctors have unique procedures to follow that give them the best chance to help a patient recover, they don't always succeed. That is why trying to heal a person with Reiki does not diminish their ability to help people heal.

In addition, signs of Reiki are things you really need to avoid to become a Reiki Master. If you can run your energy naturally if your hands get warm, and you have had a positive effect on others through hand-in-hand healing or remote healing, the signs of Reiki and becoming a Reiki master can only help you become a stronger healer. Perhaps this knowledge can encourage you to know more about Reiki and all the advantages that it not only gives how you hear but also how this can change your life positively.

CHAPTER THREE

Reiki Seichem Healing Benefits

What are Seichem and Reiki?

Reiki and Seichem are healing processes that work through the hands of the practitioners by canalizing energy into the body. While emotional and psychological healing is more correlated than physical illnesses, collective thinking is to have good internal health if one wishes to be safe on the outside and based on this principle, both Reiki and Seichem will cure physical illnesses as well as emotional diseases.

From where does Reiki come?

Reiki is a long-standing practice in Asian communities for the treatment of current diseases and the prevention of further illnesses. Reiki is also related to some branches of traditional Chinese medicine due to its roots in Japan.

Reiki's real history was somewhat concealed in the myth, and the facts possibly will never be fully known. Documentation currently available suggests Dr. Mikao Usui has created Reiki on Mount Kurama, one of many sacred mountains in Japan, for a 21-day fasting and meditation practice in solitude. Recently this data was only available in Japan, and it is not clear how accurate this story is. How does Reiki work?

Reiki is one of a variety of alternative therapies, similar to reflexology and acupuncture, based on various points of the body. All these holistic, energy-based therapies are driven on the body 's' chakra' or auras, and all of them are very close to one another and based on ancient Asian theories. The main difference is that while reflexology operates by massaging or exerting pressure on the different energy points and acupuncture involves injecting needles into various positions, and the practitioner does not necessarily involve the client.

Instead, energy is aimed at the points of the body by putting the hands gently on or just over several places on the body of the recipient. The energy flows directly through the practitioner into the recipient's body through points, but is not generated by the practitioner and doesn't absorb the Reiki practitioners ' supplies of energy. Advanced doctors may even take medication remotely, also if it is incredibly sophisticated, and should not be attempted by new doctors.

Who can give Reiki treatment and receive it?

Practicing Reiki does not require special skills or years of study. You should learn to treat Reiki yourself, your parents, friends, animals, and plants. Some may even use Reiki on tools. It is, therefore, fair that a healing process that uses pure energy heals and eliminates inefficiencies when such organisms. Everything in the world operates with some form of energy.

Everyone can canalize specific healing energy but remains unconscious until one can awaken this ability through an initiation process called attunement. Everyone can be tuned, regardless of their age or other factors, and learn how to channel Reiki successfully. A professional Reiki master performs atonement, and you can practice Reiki and share the benefits with others and treat yourself once you have been tuned. Nonetheless, when treating a patient, Reiki will stabilize, energize, and cure a practitioner.

What are Reiki's unique advantages?

Reiki can help relieve pain and sickness, be it physical, psychological, mental, or religious. This means necessarily that Reiki can heal. The disease occurs when the mind, body, and spirit become imbalanced. Emotional problems and physical disorders are caused by disturbances in the field of personal energy, and real well-being can be achieved only by restoring the whole being to harmony and balance not just with itself but also with Earth and the Universe. Reiki is one of the easiest ways to restore balance and harmony.

As a comparison to more traditional Western medicine, which is only used for the treatment of specific problems during pain and under the supervision of a physician, Reiki can be used daily. Reiki helps, of course, the recovery of patients who receive medical treatment, but can also be used to prevent disease. Since a lack of control causes the illness, it can only be a good practice to preserve oneself at all times and thus reduce the risk of becoming sick. Some think Reiki therapy is such a pleasant experience that it is a soothing and calming procedure to take part in regular sessions, as well as massages or facials, guided viewing sessions.

What does Reiki do correctly?

Reiki releases suppressed body and mind power, which facilitates relaxation and stress reduction. Natural energy has an innate intelligence, no matter where the treatment is performed on the skin, automatically re-directs and goes wherever it is required, helping to cleanse the body of toxins. Reiki also works on plants, animals, and even specific machines.

We continue the healing process by acting on our desire to be safe and whole. We can't get well without the drive to be successful. Reiki is a way to empower and allow us to be full in every way. When Reiki is provided, it enhances the energy flow through your aura and into your physical body. Reiki energy works to harmonize or put into harmony all of you, including your physical, psychological, cognitive, and spiritual parts, that makeup you as a whole. Reiki removes psychological barriers and pain, as well as power blocks within other aspects of' you,' ensuring that you stay physically and emotionally balanced and safe, both inside and outside.

Is there any proof that Reiki is working?

Scientists and doctors are somewhat unwilling to accept the legitimacy of energy healing practices. Research has, however, consistently demonstrated a substantial and rapid change in health after many different forms of energy care. Aura photographs also showed significant differences before and after Reiki treatments.

This is no guarantee that someone will be healed of any issues with one or more Reiki sessions, and Reiki should never be used as a replacement for professional medical care, particularly if they suffer from severe illness. In most cases, however, Reiki seems to improve the benefits of preventive care for tandem with it, as well as the natural ability of the body to heal itself, and patients seem to recover faster and more fully while undergoing medical treatments and Reiki together. Reiki has the fundamental principle that it can do no good and can not be used for any negative reason, so doing something that could improve one's healing cannot harm.

While the use of Reiki in the treatment of illness and injury may be controversial, Reiki is generally accepted and commonly used as an approach of relaxation and stress reduction. Reiki enhances other bodywork and techniques for recovery, sports performance, and spiritual development.

Seichem's implementation is so close to Reiki that there is not much more to be said. It's kind of... There are four elements, earth, fire, air, and water, all of which are full of different types of energy. Reiki is just Earth power, while Seichem is exposure to all four elements which produce mixed emotions, perceptions, and all have different healing properties during treatments and initiations.

Energy healing power (Reiki) is felt as heat and cold feelings, as well as on the surface of the Earth.

Fire is clearly and instantly defined as low-voltage bursts that sound like a dry, roaring sensation.

The water feels like waves of intense energy and creates deep emotional healing problems.

Air/Ether is a dual power composed of air and spirit and is ideal for psychological healing. This increases the power of the third eye and the word spoken. In the procedure, the practitioner and the client frequently experience the presence of angels when this power is channeled.

The power that can be felt during a Seichem tuning cycle is much higher than during Reiki sessions. The room is filled with strength and comfort that can be handled physically. For a few days after initiation, a newly tuned Seichem practitioner must drink plenty of water to remove clear blockages and harmful energies from his body.

During the Reiki tuning process, the initiated person will have their vibrational energy level raised, which will enable them to have more transparent access to healing energy. The Seichem tuning process opens up a person even more and gives them a much stronger cure. Unlike Reiki, anyone can become a Seichem practitioner by starting the tuning process. The only prerequisite is that you and others want to recover both physically and emotionally.

Upon starting a new Seichem practitioner, they will have unlimited access to healing energies. They can continue to use the power to help themselves and others as long as they wish. The exorcism process seems to change people for the better, and never again are they the same. Practitioners have indicated that they feel happier and optimistic, gain new trust and suddenly find the motivation and ability to change the issues they had previously ignored in their lives.

Unlike doing Reiki, Seichem practitioners do not claim to be able to cure all ills themselves directly. We are merely a facilitator that can guide the universal energies to help the receiver recover and maintain the best possible physical and emotional health.

The Healing Breath

The Healing Air Practice expands the life force in you to heal yourself and others.

Breathing is far more than just oxygenating and blood cleansing by bringing the air in and out of the lungs. The breath is a medium to transfer hidden energies, which are called prana or life force in Indian spiritual teachings.

The Healing Atem is a pranayama form. Pranayama breathes with the specific intention of controlling the strength of life. Pranayama can also be called a breathing universe breath.

There are two sources in the word "pranayama": "prana" and "yama." "Prana" means vital energy or life force that penetrates all layers of the universe and permeates and stimulates one's body. "Yama" means control and refers to controlling life force through concentration and deliberate breath control in the word "pranayama."

By exercising the Healing Breath exercise with commitment and the right attitude, you will begin to notice positive changes in your behavior within a short period of time or weeks. The breath of healing, together with a variety of other ways of pranayama, can: ease your mind and your body, relieve stress disorders, improve the auto-function of your body, for example, digestion and elimination, temporarily or permanently relieve pain, rejuvenate your nervous system, endocrine glands, body tissues, cells, and organ, expel toxins from your body, extend life, improve the body.

Virtually everybody can do the Healing Breath exercise because it does not require special knowledge or skill and can be carried out anywhere. We need to practice it daily and have a positive attitude to be successful. The Healing Breath is not just an excellent place to begin a spiritual practice, but also an excellent place to come back for those who have studied several years without significant progress in spiritual technology. Even the followers use the calming breath to begin their training, as they know that it will rapidly calm the mind and prepare the way for deep meditation. I use it before meditation to self-heal and to calm my mind.

It is very difficult to get deep in the meditation until full control of the breath is achieved, and you can become frustrated in your efforts and disappointed with your path.

EFFECTS from Healing Breath: Changes in any aspect of our interconnected physical, emotional, and religious structure are affected. Every other aspect of our process is affected by changes in one component. Our breathing affects our physical, mental, and spiritual state and vice versa.

PRECAUTIONS: If the cardiopulmonary system has a physical condition, a doctor should be consulted before attempting the exercise. Please also note that breathing is an automatic, autonomous nervous system controlled process. Usually, you don't have conscious control over it, and if you try to control it actively, you will fight the needs of the body. Caution should, therefore, be used. When dealing with your breathing pattern, always do what comes naturally and without force. When you start feeling dizzy, you may have to breathe slowly or stop breathing.

PHYSICAL EFFECTS: Daily healing exercises bring beneficial changes to all aspects of our body-mind-mind. As the mind is relaxed by the slow breathing, the brain and glands are able to control chemicals that regulate our biochemistry: we sleep better, our overall mood improves, and we become less nervous. Furthermore, muscle relaxation, reduced pain, strengthened cardiovascular and pulmonary systems, increased physical endurance and resilience, improved digestion, and increased concentration and problem-solving capabilities. Tobacco dependence (or other drugs) or cravings of any kind can be spread and ultimately removed if the treatment is performed correctly and consistently. We can have deep meditations easier. It takes just a few days to start realizing these effects.

Mental EFFECTS: Our mental structure is based upon our self-created ego. When the ego is upset or challenged, we can become angry and lose focus, too. Then the breath gets quick and shallow. The process of removing ego will trigger this upheaval in us, as we threaten our ego with the prospect of death, and the ego fights ferociously. This can be experienced during meditation as a busy mind.

Before working with a healing customer, I used to address my ego with eagerness by saying,' Well, ego, get out. You can come back later, but be gone now.' I now order it to leave, now, because if we allow the ego's wish to exist, we give up control over our lives and remain stunned within the boundaries of the false domain ego.

We invite the ego to leave when we start the healing breath exercise, and we have to realize that the ego is able to defend its condition by making us doubt or feel anxious or restless. We need to be armed with the power of reality and inner calm to conquer the false beliefs of the ego. The only force that the ego cannot withstand is our right to determine what we know best, and as our breath grows longer and deeper, we are in a calm, comfortable state of consciousness. A new understanding emerges with continuing training, which can recognize and extinguish any unwelcome mood with marginal efforts.

SPIRITUAL EFFECTS: By nature, we are all spiritual beings, so in fact, there is nothing that we can learn from doing a healing breath, which we already have. What we do becomes mindful of our ancestral spiritual state. Through regular practice, the disturbances of shape, sound, smell and taste, touch, and thinking can vanish, and we can quiet the busy mind and relax the body, heal ourselves and others and suddenly realize our pure, non-dualist existence as a spirit. Then we know that in Divine Love, everything is one. To Heaven. By Christ. When that happens, we lose all ego memory and are free.

BREATH PATTERN The following patterns are natural breathing: 1.inhalation 2. Retain (retention of the breath) 3. Exhalation 4. Exhalation 4. Retention (stopping the breath) Usually only takes a moment after each inhalation and exhalation. However, if the mind is constantly fixed on the inhaled energy (life force) spreading within the organism, the retention will naturally be extended for longer and longer periods.

My method of activating the healing breath is as follows. You can first practice hatha yoga.

THE BREATH HEALING PART ONE

- Set an intention to allow the breath of healing. Tell your ego. Order your ego to go.
- Say a prayer that is free to embrace spiritual healing.
- Quiet yourself. Quiet yourself. Be relaxed. Be confident. Close your eyes. Close your eyes.
- Take a deep breath and relax it. Drop your back. Lower your head.
- You have to clear your aura: a. Driveaway negative energy or you attached people, b. Build a safety bubble around you, c. Prepare for breath, healing, meditation. Prepare.
- Concentrate for a while on your usual rhythmic nose breathing. Relax your heart. Calm your

mind. When you think of something other than your body, remove your consciousness and peacefully return to watch your breath stream.

- Keep focusing on your breath. Relax and take a deep breath. Fill the belly and expand the air into the ribs and chest during each inhalation, and then allow the belly to join during each exhalation. This is the healthiest way we can breathe. When fully relaxed, we do it automatically.

- Listen to your breathing sound. Feel your breath when it enters your body and leaves it.

- 9 As you move to do this, relax, and feel the air as it fills the entire body. Each small cell seems to fill this prana, soaking in soothing light while holding the breath in a state of rest, not pressing it to stay.

- Sprinkle very slowly and softly; relax. There is a sense of calm because the sensation of exhalation is good.

Many times repeat steps 9 and 10.

With each long, healing breath and energy that comes from the spinal centers (chakras), the whole energy that is brought into the body is now dispersed throughout the body, moving through the subtle energy channels. The increase in energy and oxygen that stream in the soothing, meditative silence when you practice this technique even nourish the brain twice. This is a healing therapy at every stage. It creates a healthy, peaceful state and nourishes our body, mind, and soul while opening up more doors for knowledge and spiritual consciousness.

TWO HEALING BREATH OF PAIN OR DISCOMFORT

Continues from PART ONE

1. Start from PART ONE 1. When you breathe in, scan your body for any pain or discomfort that needs to be cured.

2. When you catch your cleansing breath, send the energy of healing to this particular area or the whole body, and let it stay, or ask God to send the energy of healing, where you need it.

3. Breathe out. Breathe out. Relax. Relax. Slowly release tension and make pain comfortable.

4. Always, inhaling, transferring power to the same part of the body you know needs to be healed or to let its whole body live.

5. Breathe out of that area or the entire body. Push the issue out or the discomfort. Feel or imagine the air leaving your body to take the question.

6. Repeat until you feel that this area is finished.

Go to another area where healing may be needed. End with a spirit, thanks to you.

Start from PART ONE

1. PART THREE HEALING BREATH for HEALING Other Continue Ask for healing for the highest benefit of the person or situation.
2. Breathe in and catch the breath of regeneration, exhale, hold it. Repeat. Repeat.
3. Feel your breath slower and create energy within.
4. Fill your heart with healing energy with every slow breath intake. Send your uplifted hands with this power.
5. Release the energy slowly by breathing your arms, towards a person or situation, for a cure.
6. See how healed the person or condition is.

Keep going until you believe you're done. Start with a spirit, thanks to you.

EF It's going to be of great benefit if you can practice the soothing breath quickly, without pain or difficulty. It can be used to improve overall well-being and to address specific conditions. It can be used at any distance for self-healing or healing others.

The exercise of a healing breath is easy to master if you take time every day. In the letters from Christ, Jesus said to me many times, "Practice, practice, practice." It could take you many months to feel the power that affects your body. I use these techniques when I wake up in the morning, but they can be done anywhere at any time.

You will be able to develop your ability to understand and feel differently by practicing the healing breath. When the Healing Breath is triggered, it causes the chakras to be simultaneously opened, resulting in a state of deep relaxation and peace that helps you to reach a higher level of consciousness.

Suggestion: In hatha yoga, relax while you keep every pose in steps 9 and 10 of Part One.

What Does Spiritual Treatment Mean?

Spiritual healing is an essential work that allows people to overcome their root causes problems in the spiritual realm. However, without knowing and adhering to the principles of this basic science, spiritual healers can harm the practice of spiritual healing. The most enduring method of spiritual healing helps the troubled person to begin his spiritual practice and continue it.

I. What is a religious cure?

Spiritual research by the SSRF has shown that up to 80 percent of the problems in life have their roots in the spiritual dimension. Religious healing, as described by SSRF, overcomes religious causes of issues.

II. Difference between the symptoms shown and the root cause The symptoms exhibited by an individual should be distinguished from the fundamental root cause. We can understand this better by example.

Let's say if she's not there, John throws a bucket of water on the floor of Jane's place. Instead, he hides to watch the reaction of Jane as she returns. When Jane enters the room, she searches the cause high and low, but can't find the groundwater. Instead, she wipes the floor. John lets out an evil laugh at Jane's frustration and ignorance of the root cause with his heart.

This is a typical example of how a religious motive, like a fantasy attack (John), can trigger a lifetime issue like a heart condition (i.e., rain on the ground). As we do not have the sixth sense ability to see or hear the ghost, we are only confined to the physical or psychological aspect of our quest for the origin of, say, chest pain.

III. Who causes Spiritual Healing?

We can now understand that medical or surgical inter-vention can only reduce the resulting damage done by spiritual root cause in cases of heart disease arising from a religious root cause. Therefore, medical science can at best bring about asymptomatic cure by treating the heart by surgery or medication. However, the disorder persists as the root cause, such as the ghost, is not discussed.

Supernatural healing involves diagnosing and eliminating the supernatural root cause of the problem, that is to say, the ghost of the heart disease example above. It could also be used in the first place to stop a potential problem.

While advanced spiritual healing solutions can also undo physical damage done, it is typically best to use medical interventions (treatment) to minimize physical damage. This is because you should use plenty of spiritual energy to do what you can do at a physical level with comparatively less input. This is considered to be invaluable and extremely difficult to gain mental power relative to any physical effort.

That is why the Spiritual Science Research Foundation (SSRF) emphasizes that only the right amount of energy should be used to deal with a problem. For example, if a person has eczema due to a spiritual root cause, drugs must be used at a physical level, and religious root cause must be alleviated.

IV. Fundamental Principles behind spiritual healing. Diagnostic law A problem with its root cause in the spiritual realm can only be diagnosed in the sixth sense

(ESP). The exactness of a diagnosis can vary considera-
bly and depend on two fundamental factors: the ability
and spiritual level of the sixth sense of the individual
(ESP) compared with the strength of the deity or ghost
(demon, devil, spirit, etc.), the fate of the person that determines the period of suffering Resolve the guiding
saint b. The concept behind any kind of spiritual healing
This is the concept behind any form of spiritual healing
in the world.

We seek ultimately to decrease the subtle elements of
raja-tama induced by the ghosts by applying spiritual
healing remedies Seek to erase or at least reduce the layer
of black power produced by ghosts, which is inherently
raja-tama.

(Sattva (pure, divine), raja (action, passion) and tamas
(ignorance and inertia) are the essential subtle elements
of creation made of and not yet' discovered' in modern
sciences)

V. Standard forms of spiritual healing methods Two conventional spiritual healing methods are available. Those
two options refer to us all who have an issue in the spiritual realm that has its root cause.

Religious remedies: Whether someone else or the person
himself is working to relieve a particular issue at a spiritual level.

Spiritual practice: when an individual performs spiritual practice following the five fundamental principles of spiritual practice, he develops his ability to protect himself against harmful components in the spiritual dimension. The first healing approach generally produces symptomatic healing and sometimes cures the spiritual root cause, and then heals the root cause of a religious one.

VI. Modes of spiritual healing: The healing energy is produced: the use of inanimate objects such as holy water or holy ash.

By a person (usually a person must be over 50% religious) Through a priest, i.e., a person above the spiritual level of 70%.

(This spiritual degree is defined on a 0% to 100% scale where inanimate objects would be at 0% and where a God-Realized Soul would be at 100%, i.e., someone who has fused with a God Principle) The process of action, i.e., how energy is channeled changes depending on the model used.

VII. The spiritual level of spiritual healers is the all-important aspect that defines: How you can treat others. What healing methods you can use and the kinds of universal energy that you have access to

VIII. Forms of Healing: Examples of different techniques for spiritual healing often used to cure others can be chanting the name of the Lord: chants to others are only available when you have a minimum spiritual level of 37% and are the best way to help others.

Prayers and surrender: we accept our inability to fix an issue as we pray. This abandonment of the problem often helps to reduce our ego and, thus, a temporary spiritual increase. In this way, we can reach the power of the spirit, which transfers energy to others behind our prayer. That's why our healing prayers work for others.

Religious methods of healing: an ethical way of healing such as Pranic and Reiki, use the power of the mind, enhanced by the Divine Power of the Will. This kind of spiritual healing can be done only by an individual at about 50% of the spiritual level. We have no access to universal vital energy. Vital energy exists only on an individual level, not on a broad scale. When you have access to mind power, you can regulate the vital energy in the actual body.

A person below the 50 percent spiritual level cannot theoretically recover by these methods. This is because they have inadequate access to fundamental energies. If a person under the spiritual level of 50% can render seemingly miraculous cures using Pranic healing or Reiki, it is always ghosts that heal through. Such healers are used by spirits to influence society. While temporary relief or miracle recovery from a problem can occur, hallucinations use the faith in the healer to infuse people with dark energy and distract people.

IX. What is the catalyst for spiritual energies?

The critical factor in deciding whether a person can recover based on the amount of spiritual practice and the accompanying spiritual level. This spiritual practice can be either this or an earlier lifetime.

The desire for healing is a secondary factor that contributes to the capacity of a spiritual healer to heal.

X. How do you know if you need spiritual healing?

Spiritual research carried out by the SSRF over the last 20 years has revealed that 80 percent of life's problems have a root cause in the spiritual dimension. So these issues can be overcome entirely only by supplementing global efforts in the spiritual dimension with remedies. It illustrates the profound significance of spiritual healing in the resolution of life's problems.

With the aid of the intellect, it is difficult to decide if one has to improve spiritual practice with other spiritual remedies. Only the Saints and those with an ESP or sixth meaning could say with authority whether it is necessary to have a spiritual healing remedy because they can only diagnose whether the spiritual root causes the problem.

But a decision based on your mind can also be taken if the following are observed: issues which do not go away despite the best practical efforts.

No apparent reason for chronic or persistent issues.

Problems that affect many people in a family at the same time.

Problems that exacerbate the moon and full moon.

Problems that are at least partially alleviated if the affected person is exposed like in the company of the saints to a spiritually positive environment.

Also, spiritual practice, a kind of spiritual cure, should be performed daily.

XI. Can one suffer in any situation if spiritual healing is wrong?

The short reply is yes. Some of the ways it can be detrimental are as follows: healers seeking fame and fortune, and the lower religious stage are more often affected by illusions. Such flaws and associations in the spiritual healer are used by higher-level spirits to influence and control them. The healer would not have the slightest indication that a spirit possessed him. The influence was subtle and invisible. That's why it's unnoticed. Once they have had the healer, they at first ease the symptoms of those treated by the healer by their spiritual strength, so that they may retain their faith, but also infuse the prescribed person with black energy.

If the healer has no advanced sixth sense, he cannot distinguish in the implicit universe the difference between positive and negative. Therefore, while the healer may believe he channels spiritual guides ' energy, he is healed by black power from the spirit guides. Even if the initial symptoms are treated to gain trust, the long-term effects are quite adverse.

XII. Who are we to heal, and when are we to recover?

We need to recognize two essential principles at the outset.

Spiritual healing is best when a person practices spiritual healing. This way, you build up your useful resources so that you are less likely to attack the spiritual dimension. Regular spiritual practice is also much more effective as a measure of security than the temporary cure of some form of spiritual healing. Spiritual healers will empower people to begin their spiritual practice and to be routine even though they continue to come for healing. The spiritual practice supports the efforts of the spiritual healer to eradicate the problem.

Spiritual development is our essential purpose in life to understand Christ. Accordingly, if we are all working to support ourselves and others to succeed spiritually, spiritual healing, or otherwise, we profit maximally.

Despite the above, the time and energy of spiritual healers are best spent by helping others to conquer any religious obstacles that impede their spirituality. They help people to grow spiritually in this way. From a purely spiritual point of view, people who do not intend to start spiritual practice shouldn't use spiritual healing energies. This is because, without spiritual practice for enhanced spiritual healing, the affected entity can at best cause temporary relief as harm in other areas of life or the victim can be harmed by other entities repeatedly. Spiritual healers have access to their religious level-appropriate universal energy. There is a responsibility to help people to develop spiritually that is in line with our life purpose. If this is not the case, the spiritual healer continues to stagnate and continually deteriorate in his spiritual level.

It is best not to get healing people emotionally carried away purely for healing's sake. If there is a certain amount of pain in one's life, all we do is momentarily relieve it. But the individual must still go through the necessary suffering quota. It would rather be more correct spiritually if our purpose were to cure a person so that he may have faith that the spiritual dimension exists, and that, in effect, encourages him to continue his spiritual practice.

Conclusively, many people worldwide practice spiritual healing. They can only be sure of harmony with the purpose of life by knowing the values and divine possibilities of' who' and when' to heal. The best gift that you can offer to others is to help you start your spiritual practice so that you can improve yourself.

The Chakras Spiritual Development

The human being has three bodies: a physical body and its consciousness; the astral body or subtle body that has been experienced as feelings and emotions. The seventh chakras are the ghostbusters of power for the 3 bodies / mentes, each of which governs various functions. As each chakra is triggered, the body/mental is cleaned, and the mind is spiritualized. Energy shifts slowly from darkness, the negative pole into the light, the positive pole, and the seven chakra's total consciousness. The method was associated with western psychoanalysis.

FIRST CHAKRA

Muladhara is a negative polar, at the coccyx. You are married to establishment principles at this stage. Security and autonomy are the predominant topics. Primitive energies such as terror, battle, and flight are prevalent responses to physical or psychological assault or injury. You are experiencing intense global anxiety, which threatens to destroy. This chakra is related to anxiety, dependence, and extreme illness, which can contribute to violence. Those worries are latent in the average person, but they may still affect your life. Where these desires are denied, they are projected as hurtful onto others. As these fears are conscious, incorporated, and transmuted, development starts. If unconscious impulses or memories are brought into conscious awareness, more energy for greater functioning is made available.

When the sleeping snake gradually wake up, you may feel the floating, happy, tingling, and warmth feeling at the base of the spinal cord. Vision or clairaudience may appear.

THE SECOND,

Svadhisthana is below the naval and the genitals. The second is Svadhisthana. Your senses and your nervous system are increasingly sensitive to your physical and emotional problems. The focus is not on defensive self-protection, but more on sexual and sensual pleasures. Therefore it is more interactive with others, although as sexual objects and a wider range of emotions, although unconscious impulses and appetites continue to control you. These procreative energies are quite influential, when you are not articulated, sublimated, or upwardly guided, they can be very painful physically and mentally. Meditation and tantric sexual practices offer ways to channel the Kundalini to higher levels.

This chakra is seen as the seat of the unconscious, and once opened, you may be overwhelmed with intense, sometimes conflicting emotions. All of your past conditioning and habits are exposed and conducted, and the Kundalini descend if not studied or done with increasing awareness. Only after the private unconscious has been effectively investigated and incorporated will higher transpersonal consciousness levels be achieved. There are warnings that if you don't have enough ego strength, character, and faith in God, the energies that are released can cause great harm to the individual, whether from inadequate romantic or sexual attaches to mental disintegration. This chakra awakens awareness of the astral body and the increased power of intuition. Spontaneous telepathic encounters and prophetic visions also occur.

The sixth, Manipura, is similar to the solar plexus. Power and energy and the need to fulfill your personal needs in the world are all problems here. The challenge is to make a difference in the world without dominating, controlling, or submitting to others. Once Manipura is awoken, you are aware of your spirit, gain control of emotions, and thus power beyond your own karma. Many cultures consider this as the start of spiritual evolution, as Kundalini continues to descend unless you have survived the difficulties of the second chakra. You may also encounter digestive problems here as the body is cleansed. There are more ESP capabilities.

The FOURTH CHAKRA

The fourth is between the nipples, or Anahata or Heart Chakra. You are when Anahata is completely awakened, you're separated and transcended from your emotions. Feelings are less polluted by addictions and desires. You know your emotions and karma, but you can practice your free will to fulfill your desires. Now the soul will direct your choices and actions more fully. With basic instincts and conditions for survival weakened (in the first three chakras), energy is required to concentrate on self-fulfillment. This chakra is therefore believed to be the crossroads between the earthly and the divine and the left (yin) and right (yang). The symbol of the cross and also the six-pointed star consisting of two triangles reflect this. Your mind is in the spiritual world, more and more.

In the heart area, you can experience stabbing pains. This is finally followed by the abandonment of the fight for control and the readiness to be directed by the soul more and more. In the Jungian context, the ego and the self have greater harmony and relation. As a consequence, there is less internal tension, more peace with yourself and others, and less misunderstanding and division between good and evil. As you get more integrated and full, others are less attached and requested and more alert, sensitive, and respectful of others. You should give without obtaining or exploiting others for personal gratification. A positive outlook towards life grows, which is considered essential to sustaining the evolution of Kundalini. Psychokinetic and healing forces emerge, and the realization of the synchronicity and the desire starts.

The fifth, Vishuddhi, is on the throat and thyroid gland. Vishuddhi is linked to soulful creativity and language. It requires the ability to put the ego aside and to convey the higher self or creative intellect mentally and artistically. The throat chakra likewise regulates the ability to receive nutrition from others and the divine. Gradually, you achieve a sense of confidence and security, knowing that an internal transpersonal source emanates unlimited sustenance. Through engaging the mysterious and trustful spirit, you nourish yourself in the making. You start to work more and more in the universe, linked to the spiritual realm.

It is also said that this core governs our sense of space and time, whether we experience time slowly or quickly, and it determines our life's rhythm. Hearing can sharpen, and telepathic powers eventually develop.

SIXTH CHAKRA The sixth chakra, Ajna, is located between the pineal and hypophysical eyebrows. Sight and light are associated with the pineal gland. You can see the light around the forehead when this chakra is triggered. Intelligence and insight are improved. You should contact your superior wisdom or mentor. The inner vision obtained brings you beyond the physical dimension and beyond time, space, and causality limitations. You feel connected to nature and the entire universe. This wisdom represents a union of two types of intellectual and sentimental knowledge. The two lines left and right, woman and masculine, enter the caduceus chakra of Ajna.

SEVENTH The seventh, Sahasrara, is the positive pole at the top of its head. The Door of Brahman opens, and the divine power, symbolized by a crown, halo or light, enters if Kundalini triggers this chakra. First of all, you have nausea and brief periods of samadhi; it stimulates all the other chakras further. Duration and effects increase with practice. When you are fully active, duality disappears, and you achieve cosmic consciousness, samadhi, or illumination. God is perceived as a being; subconscious emotions or thoughts no longer exist, nor is a division between self and the awareness of sensation or thought. You become pure consciousness, joy, and a profound understanding of yourself and the true nature of all life and all dimensions.

Sahasrara is in the "soft spot" that closes slowly after the spirit enters at birth and is then reopened to exist when it dies. Adepts will prepare for their time of death as their consciousness completely leaves their bodies. To protect this region, Orthodox Jews are wearing a skull cap, while some monks shave to leave it exposed.

There are many ways the chakras are awoken. A summary of tantric yoga practices is provided in Hiroshi Motoyama's Theories of the Chakras. One strategy is to look at every chakra at the top of the nose. Another practice is to imagine each chakra's associated color and sing the accompanying mantra.

The order in which the chakras awaken varies with the karma and existence of each person. Many are physically and mentally impaired by this mighty force, unable to live a normal life, and never reap the expected benefits, which is why it is important to study with an experienced teacher rather than to speed up the process.

CHAPTER FOUR

Deep Introspection Concerning
the Principles of Reiki

Anyone can adapt and learn to cure Reiki. You don't need special gifts, and you don't need to be mental. All it really needs is openness to Reiki and discipline to practice. It's important to find a good Reiki master with whom you are relaxed and strong.

Dr. Usui recommended his Reiki students frequent relaxation plus a daily knowledge of the following five values. While the concepts taught by Dr. Usui may seem very simple, as you progress your Reiki practice, it is necessary to approach them in an advanced way. Each chapter explains and interprets the Reiki concepts to your benefit and to incorporate them into your own personal transformation practice.

Today I thank you for the many blessings that Simple sounds.

This principle actually requires practice. All-important signs of gratitude consist of saying grace before dinner, offering bows to Buddhist, Hindu, or Christian symbols and praying before bedtime. Another approach is to write down everything you are grateful for in your life. Talk about these and see for yourself the amazing wealth you have got. Eventually, meditate on "thank you" and "gratitude" words and thoughts. At the same time, respect your family, your teachers, and your elders. This can be achieved through the Buddhist practice of "commitment," which at the end of each meditation is to give love and empathy to all beings. Will you know the strength of thankful awareness?

Japanese scientist Masaru Emoto experimented with water effects. The Message from Water included writing "thank you" and "love, an appreciation" on papers attached to water samples in one of his experiments. The water was then frozen and microscopically photographed. The resulting photos displayed elegant, balance, and integrity crystal structures. The same test was done; on the other hand, with the words,' you make me sick. I'll kill you.' These specimens are skewed, scattered, and evidently unhealthy in their crystal images. Such experiments show that water reacts to human consciousness and speech. The water experiments actually represent the importance of appreciation in our daily lives and in our practice of Reiki. Picture the thoughts and words ' impact on a wider scale. I suggest you check Emoto's research and photos to see his spectacular findings. The photographs of crystals can also help you understand quantum physics in a strong visual way. Then you can judge the force of consciousness for yourself. Let's now move on to Reiki's second concept.

I'm not going to worry today.

Don't worry! Instead, Easier said he did. To arrest anxiety requires strong attention during the worrying process. Take careful note of the motion of your thoughts during your meditation and focus. Whenever an issue emerges, recognize it and consider its existence. Be kind to your concerns; do not chase, refute, or hide them. Alternatively, try to understand the essence of your problems and how they affect you. Your concerns exist for some purpose in your mind. Your questions may have served you very well on security or identification sometimes. The question remains, are your fears representing your best interests, or are they back in a lifetime? Monitor your thoughts and see which are irrelevant and which are helpful to your well-being. Determine if your issues are your own or if your community or family may have inherited them. Carefulness lets you know your issues well without falling prey to them.

Today, I won't be angry.

This Reiki principle is also quite easy, as long as all goes well. Be mindful that you feel anger in your chest. See how you will keep your eyes on a medium dog. Be friendly to him, don't turn your back on him and don't threaten him, but be alert to his danger. Wrath and paranoia no longer need to exist with true understanding. Finally, catch the frustration before it turns into words; suppress it before it is full-blown. True knowledge penetrates the root of every cause. Anger reveals a deeper part of your life perspective. It can be rooted in righteous outrage, unexplained terror, or commonplace discrimination. Observe and grasp your anger in politics. Decide whether they are an essential part of your being, useful feelings to know the truth of your mind or dangerous unconscious responses that kill your peacefulness. Consciousness through meditation will aid you tremendously in this process. Thich Nhat Hanh, the venerable Zen Buddhist monk, explains that irritations can be understood with a few gentle breaths to turn it into something more meaningful such as understanding and affection. He states that wrath and concern are destructive energy. Whether you are talking about science or spirituality, it is impossible to destroy energy. All you can do is make it more constructive.

Forgiveness is constructive energy, like love. When you're upset, it's like a light that shows you how to forgive. If you choose, you should hang on to your frustration on the premise that anger is as normal as everything else. In reality, within us, all naturally exist rage, fear, resentment, and jealousy. The task of meditation is to raise awareness of all sentiments. You build a good sense of all the emotions through consciousness, not just the bad ones. The difference is that positive emotions are healthy and nutritious, and negative emotions are harmful. Wholeness comes when you strive with everything you have to turn negative energies into something constructive by looking at the essence of your emotions honestly and by overcoming ignorance.

Today I am genuinely doing my job.

How can you improve your dedication to this principle? See yourself all day long to make sure that you behave, speak, and think honestly. Continue to observe until you find actions or thoughts which are not truthful. That is, be frank to yourself if you find a sense of dishonesty. Then work with yourself and find ways to cleanse your thoughts before they turn into dishonest words or actions. Bhava Ram says, "When we develop ourselves securely in the facts, we don't need to worry about continuing deceit... We're moving away from ignorance and closer to the Divine." One way to test your own integrity is to examine your own self next time you question your mate. Catch yourself before criticism spills from your mouth and remember, "He may have his flaws and faults, but what are my own weaknesses and shortcomings?" Pausing to ask this question strengthens your self-confidence, knowledge of yourself, and sincerity. It allows you also to have more empathy for your mate. Similarly, when you next complain about government officials, ask yourself, "in what way do I personally contribute to government lies and corruption?" First, it disarms and exchanges criticism for a personal mirror. It challenges you to check before you blame someone else. Once you have studied your own honesty and integrity, assess the government or other criticism carefully.

Today I will be kind to my neighbors and every living thing.

The Reiki theory calls on you to open your heart even further and find a kind word and a smile for your people. Speak softly and be mindful of your words ' impact on others. That idea also helps you in evaluating your diet and whether you lead a healthy life or not. Eating meat or animal products from cruelty or death runs counter to the spiritual practice of kindness and compassion. Look at your diet closely and see what needs to be removed and what needs to be reduced gradually.

The Powers of Reiki Therapy Explained

Reiki was first developed by Dr. Mikao Usui in Japan. He was a preacher and school teacher of the Japanese Buddhist Church. He agreed to embark on a ten-year trip to the United States for further explanation. He was disillusioned and concluded after seven years that he could not find what he was looking for, so then he came back to Japan. He was staying in a Tibetan monastery to study Buddha's life and India's Sanskrit teachings.

Dr. Usui went to Mount Kurama for 21 days, while he was fasting and exercising. Dr. Usui was later hit by a blinding ray burning into his third eye (the area in the center of the forehead over the nose bridge). This illumination was followed by a great healing work in his dream. He then learned that he could heal people through magical meditation. That was the start of Reiki. (Jesus is also believed to have used this kind of healing).

In 1926, Dr. Ushi died of a stroke. He had great success in helping many people during his lifetime. He was extremely active in his regular healings, especially following the 1923 earthquake and all the subsequent injuries. During these later years, he taught Chujiro Hayashi to be his disciples and also become a great master of painting. Chujiro carried out the teachings and remedies after Dr. Usui's death and incorporated such hand movements in therapy.

During the Japanese period, a lady named Hawayo Takata, who had been cared for for four months in Hayashi's clinic, was completely overwhelmed by her Reiki care. Then she was trained for several years until her great master's status was acquired. She then moved to Hawaii and opened a clinic of her own. The perceived effectiveness of therapy spread to the Western world at this time.

The granddaughter of Hawayo Takata, Phyllis Lei Furumoto, still practices Reiki today and spreads the word of her healing throughout the world today.

The name Reiki is Japanese. "Rei" is universal, and "ki" is power. We and all around us are made of the same material. Talking is energy; our thoughts and emotions are energy. If we have negative thoughts and do not let them go, we keep them inside and keep these lodges in mind as blocks. Such negativity creates a disequilibrium. Negative emotions fill the stomach and cause illness. Lifeforce energy comes from the universe source and can be used for cleaning, energizing, and rebalancing.

In order to use the energy, we need to allow this universal energy to reach the top of the head where it can go into our brain, and then flow through our hands from the body. If we open ourselves to it and believe in its presence, we all have the ability to use that power.

Reiki energy is known by centuries to be a spiritual healing medium. However, irrespective of where the energy started or how it began, it is important that no matter where you are, the outcome of that energy is always positive. The influence of Reiki will not have any adverse effects on the body of the patient. A recipient should recognize what they can do and acknowledge that power. If a person accepts Reiki's power with an open mind, only good will result.

The energy transmitted depends on the practicer of Reiki and their trust in the power of this healing art. This action requires complete relaxation and a deep focus to conduct the process and properly channel the energy. The Reiki specialist usually moves his hands slowly, placing them a few inches above the body of the receiver.

Reiki's influence has been better understood through various studies and experiments. This helps a professional to give the receiver positive energy. It has also been proven that a hands-off healing technique has the same and sometimes even more healing power than a hands-on treatment.

The transfer of energy via remote healing is also effectively controlled by qualified practitioners. Clients who have undergone this healing process have reported remarkable changes to their health conditions. More people are trying to explore the usefulness of Reiki both as a psychologist and as a client in their own lives.

A recipient need not practice the ancient curative treatment, but the recipient can recognize the difference in their body by recognizing the beauty and power of Reiki. It takes time before the process is complete, and after each rejuvenation session, patience is required. There is sufficient evidence that this therapeutic technique is more than just a placebo effect and that Reiki therapy can show significant benefits. Open yourselves to the possibilities, and you may be shocked.

Discover the Benefits of Reiki Seichem Healing

What are Reiki and Seichem?

What are they?

Reiki and Seichem are healing mechanisms that operate by transmitting energy to the body through the hands of the practitioners. While emotional and mental healing is linked more often than physical ailments, the standard plot of thinking is to be safe outside and to have good inner health, and based on that principle, both Reiki and Seichem will cure both physical and emotional ailments.

From where does Reiki come?

Reiki is an ancient tradition of Asian communities to both current cure diseases and to avoid more diseases. Based in Japan, Reiki was also related to certain branches of traditional Chinese medicine.

Reiki's modern past was somewhat shrouded by folklore, and the facts possibly will never be fully understood. The currently available information says that during a 21-day fasting and meditation practice in isolation on Mount Kurama, one of several holy mountains in Japan, Dr. Mikao Usui created Reiki. This knowledge has only recently come to light outside Japan, and it is no longer clear how accurate this claim is. However, Mrs. Hawayo Takata from Hawaii brought the Usui method of natural healing to the west initially. Throughout her family visits to Japan, Dr. Hayashi successfully treated Mrs. Takata for chronic disease in his Reiki clinic in Tokyo. Instead, she got Dr. Hayashi's reiki tunings and could practice Reiki and introduce new practitioners herself.

How's Reiki working?

Reiki is one of a number of therapeutic, reflexological and acupunctural treatments based on various points of the body. All these holistic, energy-based therapies are based on natural' chakra' or auras of the body and are all quite close to one another, and all are built on ancient Asian theories. While reflexology works by massaging or pressing various energy points and acupuncture involve inserting needles in the various points, Reiki does not necessarily involve the practitioner touching the patient at all.

Alternatively, energy is guided to the points of the body by putting the hands gently on or over a number of locations on the body of the recipient. The energy flows through the practitioner and directly into the receiver's body through the dots, but is not produced by the practitioner and does not consume Reiki's own energy supply. Advanced practitioners can even perform medication remotely, though this is an extremely advanced procedure that inexperienced practitioners should not pursue.

Who can offer Reiki care and/or obtain it?

Practicing Reiki does not require special skills or years of study to learn. You will learn to treat yourself, your family, friends, animals, and plants with Reiki. Some may even use Reiki on appliances. It is therefore rational that a healing process using pure energy can restore or repair inefficiencies in the function of organisms and artifacts of this kind.

The ability to channel unique healing energy is inherent in everybody, but it stays unconscious until you have been awoken by a method of initiation called attuning. Anyone can be tuned, regardless of age or other factors, and learn how to channel Reiki effectively. The attunement is administered by an experienced Reiki master, and you can practice Reiki and share the benefits with others and treat yourself once you are tuned. In reality, when treating a patient, Reiki will stabilize, energize, and cure a practitioner.

What are the particular benefits of Reiki?

Reiki may help alleviate distress, whether in the physical, psychological, mental, or spiritual environment, associated with pain and disease. It basically means Reiki can cure. Disease happens when the mind, body, and spirit become imbalanced. Emotional problems and physical illnesses are the consequence of disruptions in the field of personal energy, which is only possible through the restoration of harmony and equilibrium not only with itself but also with the world and the cosmos.

Reiki is one of the most efficient ways of maintaining balance and harmony.

Contrary to more traditional western medicine, which can only be used for remedies for special conditions during pain, Reiki can be used every day under the supervision of a physician. Reiki, of course, helps the healing of clinically treated patients, but it also can be used to prevent disease. Because illness is a result of the disorder, it is only possible to remain well-equilibrated at all times in order to reduce the risk of falling ill. Most people consider the Reiki therapy so enjoyable that it is used daily for a soothing and calming procedure, in the same way, that they receive a massage or a facial, a controlled visualization session.

What does Reiki do exactly?

Reiki removes trapped energy from body and mind, fosters relaxation and stress reduction. The natural energy has an innate intelligence, and the medicine doesn't matter, it will instinctively redirect itself and go wherever possible to rid the body of toxins. Reiki works on plants, animals, and even machines and other objects that are inanimate.

We start the healing process by acting in accordance with our desire to be whole. We can't be well without the drive to be successful. Reiki is a way to inspire and make us fully integrated. When Reiki is given, the flow of energy through your aura and into your physical body increases. Reiki energy works to harmonize or put all of you, including your physical, psychological, mental, and spiritual, into harmony. In other areas of' you,' Reiki frees emotional blocks and trauma as well as energy blocks so that you remain physically and emotionally a healthy and well-balanced person, both inside and outside.

Is there any evidence that Reiki is working?

Scientists and medical doctors deny the legitimacy of energy healing practices. Research has, however, also shown a major and rapid health change following energy treatments of various forms. Aura images also revealed important changes before and after Rciki therapy.

That is no guarantee that anyone with individual or multiple Reiki therapies will be relieved of any illness, and Reiki should never be used as a substitute for professional medical treatment, especially in cases of severe disease. In most cases, however, Reiki seems to increase the medical treatment effects when combined with it and the natural ability of the body to heal itself. Patients seem to recover faster and more fully when both medical and Reiki therapies are received. Reiki's basic principle is that it can not do any good and can not be used for any negative purpose, so doing something that can aid healing can not be harmful.

Whilst the use of Reiki to treat disease and injury can be controversial, the use of Reiki as a tool to calm and reduce stress is more widely accepted and widely used. Reiki improves other bodywork and techniques of healing, sport, and spiritual development.

The introduction to Seichem Seichem is so close to Reiki that not much more can be said. It's kind of... "Reiki plus+" There are four elements, Earth, fire, air, water, all of which are full of different kinds of energy. Reiki is literally the power of the Earth, and Seichem is induction in all four elements that all produce different feelings and experiences during treatments and initiations.

The healing energy of Earth (Reiki) is experienced as very different hot and cold sensations, as on the surface of the Earth.

Fire is clearly distinguished immediately as low voltage electrical pulses that sound like a hot, bustling sensation.

Water sounds like cool energy waves and generates deep emotional issues for healing.

Air / Ether is double energy consisting of air and spirit that is good for mental healing. It increases the strength of the third eye and the word spoken. When this power is channeled during recovery, the therapist and the client often have angels.

The energy that can be felt during a Seichem tuning process is much stronger than during Reiki sessions. The room is filled with power and warmth, which can be felt physically. It is important to drink plenty of water for a few days after initiation by a newly tuned Seichem practitioner to flush clear blockages and negative energies from the skin.

During the Reiki tuning cycle, the initiated person will increase their vibrational energy level, which will allow them better access to the healing energies. The Seichem tuning process opens a person, even more, giving him a significantly stronger healing ability. Unlike Reiki, anyone can become a Seichem practitioner by starting the tuning process. The only need is to help you and others recover physically and emotionally.

After the initiation of a new Seichem practitioner, they will have unlimited access to healing frequencies and can continue to use the energies to sustain themselves and others as long as they like. The cycle of initiation seems to change people for the better, and they are never the same again. Practitioners reported being calmer and more positive, gaining new confidence and suddenly finding incentives and the ability to change the things they had previously avoided in their lives.

Like Reiki practitioners, Seichem practitioners do not profess to heal all diseases themselves personally. These are essentially an aid to direct universal forces in order to help the user improve and preserve the best possible physical and emotional health.

Long Distance Reiki Energy Healing - The Science Behind It

Absent or Remote Healing is becoming the new motto, as the Age of Water is actually ascending. People wonder what that is and whether it is really possible to actually heal Reiki energy or is it just a weird pocus scam? Some of you may have learned of remote Healing, while others call it remote Healing. Others find long-distance Healing or absent Healing, but all define one thing and fulfill the same purpose, whatever it is.

The objective of remote or absent Healing is to offer individual holistic wellbeing that can be combined with medicine in a natural and gentle way. It is known as an alternative method to medicine, even without healing from a distance.

How does remote Healing or remote healing work?

Naturally, our physical bodies produce an abundance of energy. For a simple description, our body consists of different energy levels or fields interconnecting and working together. Our energy system consists of 1.

1. Aura, or what they call the fields of energy-it to absorb and transmits power both internally and externally, and simultaneously serves as the information center for the energy of our body.
2. Chakras or just called energy centers–here, the energies obtained are broken down.
3. Meridians or energy pathways-the decomposed energies are now dispersed through the paths.

One would also appreciate the process if they realized the different energy layers in our body, or also known as the four levels that function differently:

1. Etheric field-the first energy surface associated with the "real" and which is 1/4 to 2 inches from the body;
2. Etheric field Emotional field-associated with feelings and energy stretches through the body from one to three inches deep;

3. 3 — cognitive field-linked to mental processes and our thought 3-8 centimeters outside our physical body; and,

4. The spiritual domain is the most complex because it consists of more layers that allow us to enter spiritual dimensions. This is possible when you pray or meditate.

You should collaborate with an energy healer to develop all these areas for holistic wellbeing, mobile, or remote Healing. When they already have a radiating Reiki energy flowing through them, the healers think the person recovers and transfers Universal Energy to the customer by releasing energy through his / her hands with the help of a calming mind. The range is not an impediment in terms of energy transfer or sending since energy vibrates and flows everywhere.

How Remote Healing works in relation to time, space, and energy Few of us can truly understand how remote or remote Healing can be linked to time, space, and energy — and how it works. This is because we do not know that each of us is one with the universe. Science can already explain why the distant Healing has succeeded in using energy, distance, and space on the assumption that everything in this magnificent universe is interconnected.

Take the example of satellite dishes first. Energies are transferred to create or emit signals over short or long distances. Similarly, this concept is used to describe the long-distance and Remote Healing. There are different forms of energy because the physical body has different energy fields. Now in Healing, the physical energies of an individual can be transferred to another person to heal every physical, mental, emotional, or spiritual need or concern, even when at every distance.

Since the discovery of the benefits and efficacy of far-off and remote Healing, several scientific studies have determined whether everything is real or just a hoax. A major 20th-century study led to the discovery and explanation of a field of science-quantum physics. This took place in 1982 when an experiment was conducted by a team of physicists headed by Alain Aspect at the University of Paris. The results showed that the electrons would bind instantly, although at a massive distance. It simply states that distance is not a problem if these subatomic particles are to be interconnected. This study was even duplicated and confirmed by Nicolas Gisin's findings in 1997. He also found the same result and conclusion that particles can communicate and connect under certain conditions at 20,000 times the speed of light.

It is with this deeper and scientific knowledge that we understand that remote Healing is possible as energy is transmitted and obtained from a distance, close or far since we are all linked together.

What are Reiki Healing's advantages?

Over the last few years, Reiki Healing has had an amazing, wonderful, and positive impact on millions of people. Those who took Reiki healing sessions or courses-personally with the energy cures or distance healing-claimed that they felt something else and improved their overall wellbeing. Clearly, as with any procedure, each individual patient has different experiences and consequences, as they have various problems or need Healing.

Remote Healing not only works with one particular aspect of the individual but also improves on other areas—energy healing works to heal the root of the problem and not only the symptoms. In addition to being free from tension and anxiety, people feel a lighter and more relaxed state of life. More than a healthy body with a long-range recovery, it helps them to become conscious of their inner self and eventually to be fulfilled and happy, which leads to a refreshed, rejuvenated and motivated person achieving a degree of happiness and enlightenment.

Many positive effects of remote Healing include clearness, focus, stress management, creativity, motivation, tolerance, enjoyment, enhanced mood, and vitality. In other words, people are whole in the sense that their wellbeing in all aspects is improved: physical, psychological, emotional, and spiritual.

CHAPTER FIVE

Becoming a Powerful Reiki Master

Reiki is typically the short version of Usui Reiki Ryoho's various styles. Examples of other uses include 5239 Reiki, an asteroid named after Reiki Kushida. Usui Reiki Ryoho is neither a religion nor a belief system. However, in the proven / unproven debate, it parallels religion. The power that flows in Reiki can be felt in many respects, but can neither be confirmed nor denied. When it comes to $E = mc2$ energy, but universal energy is still in the gray area. As with religions, it leaves people in the middle, saying that all comes from people and show me evidence if you think differently. A lot of ducks were produced to clarify what could not be proved.

The first law of thermodynamics states that the energy cannot be created nor destroyed; only from one shape to another can it be modified. The spiritual practice that Mikao Usui has developed uses a gentle form of universal energy, which is strong unless it is changed by human actions or other energies.

Synergism occurs when Reiki is added to other practices; since Reiki is a universal energy form, how can any additional increase it. An individual may attempt to compare Reiki with energy forms and assess its strength on a scientific scale. Or, they can just look at a child when he or she looks at a four-legged compañero who rebounds from injury and sees unproven energy coming out of the heart of that child. Reiki is the waves of love and world peace.

Even if Hippocrates did not refer to Reiki, he described its influence as' the doctor heals, but nature heals.' Surgeons and other medical professionals eradicate immediate danger, and then healing starts. It is a natural force that provides what is required to awaken and cure the inner healer. Reiki is natural power, which often helps to heal the mind and body far beyond and much faster than ever expected by any person, whether medical or otherwise. You might not find anything if you look for accurate evidence of healings directly from Reiki. Reiki teachers and practitioners focus on a way of life that best fits this form of life at that junction and need not receive praise. Komyo Reiki Kai's slogan is,' Go placidly in the midst of praise or blame.' Reiki practitioners and teachers ' bonuses are paid and overhead for the time they spend with a client or student.

Lifeforce power usually requires no evidence because every one of us encounters something. Different people used their life force power for millennia to help another person recover, sometimes being exhausted. The source of universal energy is endless. Every Reiki practitioner's energy of life force that flows through Reiki is refilled by the flow of powerful universal energy.

To become strong, different images are shown to various people. All human languages are complex and use different symbols, including letters, kanji, lines, gestures of the hand, etc. Through Reiki, we see many symbols shown to show different student energy within the particular form of universal power. The formation of symbols of Reiki was a very natural development that reflected parts of an unproved power. Often colors are used as symbols; each person's experiences decide the significance of color as a symbol. Universal energy is provided by the receptors of a person that are open to acceptance and disrupted by the elements shaping the truth of that person. Symbols, colors, and chakras are sometimes used to help students understand the flow of energy instead of trying to make universal energy stronger. Reiki is a path to peace, calmness, and happiness; you don't have to worry if symbols are not drawn exactly as shown, and symbols are transcended at the best time for each person.

To the point where humanity became strong, many "powerful" people were blessed throughout history. Imagine a woman who can be described as living in a dark silent world for a moment. Through another's teachings, she was able to have a positive effect on many lives. She became a powerful American writer who developed her discipline, determination, and time skills. "True happiness does not come from self-gratification, but from loyalty to a worthy cause." She, Helen Keller (1880-1968), writes. The historical facts of powerful people prove that their actions put them in a position of power.

There were only four years after Mikao Usui founded Reiki Ryoho his program and his death, but he gave a wonderful gift in that short time. He was a quiet man and only lifted three of his 2,000 students to the stage to open others up to the universal energy he interacted with. In 1928, Shouoh Matsui wrote, "Mikao Usui didn't like to announce" (Rivard, Doi, Inamoto, 1997-2003). (Rivard, 2003, M. Iwasaki translation) The influence of Mikao Usui is symbolized by one being the highest, a two being valued to inspire his students to do their best. Those who stand out from the crowd in history do it because their acts separate it from others.

Reiki Master portrays various levels of Usui Reiki Ryoho in different styles. Most men and women I know, despite possessing one or more Reiki Master certificates, prefer to call themselves the Reiki Shihan instructor or simply say that in another Usui Reiki Ryoho style, I've reached the fourth or higher level.

Another synonym for Master is a teacher; however, others like rule and command confuse when it comes to universal energy. Even if a person believes that all sources of universal energy in every person are misleading, if each of us is able to switch on power and control our own body completely, then we can control the degeneration and regeneration of all our cells.

The first awakening of Mikao Usui was philosophical, and he said the program he created was the path to health and happiness, after his second awakening, his relation to universal forces. What could be more effective than opening up your way to a form of universal energy which can lead to health and happiness when used in spiritual practice? The determination and discipline of some people in what is open to them seem to remove them from the position of skipper and make him or her the "Master" of their own destiny.

Not all energies are positive, even if they may feel powerful; most activities have suppositive creations. It is good to check the certificate(s) of the teacher when deciding to open your path to the universal energy called Reiki. Any Reiki teacher would be lined up back to Mikao Usui and would be happy to explain whether he or she has changed what he or she practices.

Wouldn't it be a beautiful world if instead of everybody trying to be the strongest, everybody tried to balance and allow peace to emanate from him/her? Could you imagine a world full of balance and harmony that has not heard the sound of bombs or planes that fall into the towers? As surreal as it seems now, wouldn't it be a great gift to pass on to our children and grandchildren? If the aim of each individual is to live in equilibrium in peace instead of seeking power, why not? If every section is in harmony, the whole is peaceful.

The Chakra Systems and Balancing Exercise

Many people are looking for healing strategies Some of which have been based on East (not entirely geographical) practices like Tai Chi, Chi Quong, or Yoga. In different cultures and belief systems, there are religious rituals and beliefs around the world with the same message. We can cure ourselves, we can know that, to feel that link with the universe if we can only sit still and hear our inner guidance, our inner voices.

An age of imagination and empathy is coming. Philosophy of the soul is developing. In this new age, the heart plays a major role... Healthy Heart Meditation Chakras are thought to be common in the New Age Movement to free up the toxic effects of daily stress. These energy centers will lead to a more positive balance of life and to release toxins that we produce in our daily life. Through meditation, chakras are open and relaxed to trigger this energy center. And what is chakra? What is chakra?

Chakra The word chakra comes from the Sanskrit word wheel, a spinning wheel. Some people who work with chakras will perceive any primary chakra as a spinning vortex with a particular color. In the human body, there are many chakra points, but to heal and balance, the seven main chakras are focussed on them. The seven chakras are located in ascending order along the spinal column, from the base of the spine to the top of the head.

The Root Chakra is from the lower end of the spine, about two inches underneath the belly button is the Sacred Chakra, the Solar Plexus is between the bottom of the spinal cord, in the middle, between the breasts there is the Hearts Chakra, the Throw Chakra, and the famous Third Eye between the eyes, and the Crown Chakra on the top of the head. This chapter does not aim to deal in detail with the main seven chakras. My emphasis is on the chakra of the chest.

The Heart Chakra The heart is where our emotions reside. It is weak and easy to break, but very durable. It doesn't make sense to try and deceive the heart. It depends on our honesty... The heart is the source of love, the human energy cycle. Leo Buscaglia, Does love heal everything? Who has not experienced the pain of a broken heart, sadness, and remorse, the crippling impact of deceit, emotional problems, renunciation, breakup-only to name a few in a long list of hurtful situations? The tears of a broken soul need more than physical healing. If ignored, heart pain affects the soul and consumes power, mind, body, and spirit. Medical attention is often not adequate to treat heart problems.

Believe it or not, all of us are associated with the Creator. We have the gift of perception, feeling, and awareness. We only need to learn how to tap into these gifts to see us in bad times and enjoy the good times. Is faith blind enough? Not all of us are ready to believe, much less open our minds to find that deeper link with the Divine.

In the middle of your chest is the heart chakra, in Sanskrit is Anahata Chakra, which means unstuck. It is associated with physical and spiritual self. It is the center of our physical bodies. It is among the three lower chakras that hold us in the realm of physical. chakra is the top 3 chakras, which help us develop in the spiritual realm that allows us to realize our thoughts, imagination, intuition, and creativity.

Proponents of chakra healing and balancing the power of the key chakras say that it cures pain, unlocks the intuitive abilities that we have born, calms the mind, and paves the way for inner peace. We learn how to let life flow to enjoy our countless blessings. They know that challenges and issues don't have to control our waking hours, tormenting our subconsciousness.

Through this heart chakra, we acknowledge and accept the value of the unconditional love that is available to us all. As the heart chakra grows, the other six major chakras are included. The physical and spiritual self harmonize and thus sustain life. Thinking about the chakra of the heart extends the significance of thoughts, words, and deeds-moves us to the true significance of love-universal and unconditional love.

The chakra of the heart gives us the power to live an abundant and fulfilling life. This is a guiding power that connects the physical and spiritual planes, helping us not to become self-centered, carefree, feel like a victim, and other negative attributes. The chakra of the heart is the center where we draw plenty in our lives, so as to be able to share it with others. We share a world beyond ourselves, and we are moving beyond the apparent limits of our physical world. It's easier to say than to do.

There are many meditative forms. Working with the chakras is a meditation and visualization process. There are Internet resources that offer good meditation on the heart chakra. It's a very personal choice to meditate.

Maybe not for someone else, what works for me. I advise you to use Internet power to find advice to open your chakras. Knowledge is in our possession, and no harm is done to accepted processes or values. If it doesn't work for you, no harm is done, but some information is taken away. Try to find your heart's strength! Maybe not for someone else, what works for me. I advise you to use Internet power to find advice to open your chakras. Knowledge is in our possession, and no harm is done to accepted processes or values. If it doesn't work for you, no harm is done, but some information is taken away. Try to find your heart's strength!

Reiki and Naturopathy

The profound personal transformation by Reiki reaches far beyond the treatment of individuals. The biggest causes of healing are in us as well as in the world around us. We are not only responsible for our personal health and transformation, but also for the health and development of the planet. This chapter covers nature for healing and nature for healing.

Could natural disease cure diabetes? Is it possible to cure cancer? Is blood pressure high? These questions are often heard by participants in our holistic Reiki healthcare courses. The sentence of these questions shows the pervasive philosophical influence of western allopathic medicine. That is, most people are waiting for illness and then go to a doctor to seek treatment. This is a crazy approach! Nonetheless, many people are waiting for infection instead of adopting empowerment and preventive medical practices.

This philosophy also promotes the purchase of medical insurance as if some big business might really "insure" your good health. The main thing an insurance company seeks to ensure is that year after year they make excellent profits. Does insurance make you feel safer? Could people neglect physical health on the basis of the belief that health insurance covers them? Was buying insurance really an investment in the prophecy you get sick? Does the dependence on safety insurance actually weaken your personal capacity? Naturopathy's practice circumvents most of these concerns by creating a strong synergy between you and nature.

Another type of so-called disease protection is vaccines. Although history shows that some vaccines have announced incredible health benefits, this does not indicate that all vaccines are necessary or safe; quite the opposite. Vaccine manufacturers are most certainly looking for record gain in the coming years. Do you have an interest in the pandemic spread of disease because this means incredible demand for your medicines? If you have any concerns about the profit motive, look at advertising forecasts for companies that produce vaccines for the next ten years. Look at the World Vaccine Congress, where industry leaders are discussing how the spread of disease can benefit. They go so far as to refer in their marketing lingo to "blockbuster vaccines." You will see they predict the next pandemic like goats. This is how the healthcare sector works. Naturopathy adopts an immunity strategy that is radically different.

Through trusting government and its laws, insurance companies, adjusters, or manufacturers of vaccines and their income, are you relinquishing and betraying your personal responsibility for maximizing your own health? The only genuine health insurance you can provide is a diet plan, good protection, and positive activities in all health dimensions. True immunity implies the strength and cleanliness of your whole being, not only some trendy chemicals brushing in with mercury to protect you ostensibly. Vaccines can alleviate your fear and lull you into a false sense of safety. You may not be able to really handle your own healthcare program. More seriously, some vaccines are involved in disease rather than disease prevention. Naturopathy, like Reiki, is aimed at helping you to improve and heal yourself instinctively.

Naturopathy may not cure all conditions, but proponents explain that it can most certainly prevent virtually all diseases. Naturopathy is the main point of prevention. As our Naturopathic friend Dr. Nisal explains in Pune, India, it is a way of life, not only a remedy. Naturopathy does not offer every person a standard remedy. Alternatively, it provides a plan designed to meet every person's unique needs at every stage of life. Nature is no more than uniform humans are.

In modern society, the most insightful concept I've learned from Naturopathy is the great misconception of disease. What's the misunderstanding? Allopathic western medical practice generally treats coldness, flushing, flushes, coughs, menopause, and diarrhea as diseases. In reality, these are the natural cleaning methods of the skin. Snowing, vomiting, crying, and bleeding are all perfectly ordinary detox steps that the body itself handles. In most cases, these systems can work perfectly without external intervention. The idea that these are "diseases" excuses chemical treatments in order to suppress cough, avoid a red nose or diarrhea. Virtually everyone I know deceives this belief. There are certainly cases where pharmaceuticals can be very beneficial, but they often interfere with the body's natural cleansing process. The trick is to be sufficiently informed and wise to tell when to let nature accomplish its duty and when to trust a chemical for your healing.

As drug chemicals accumulate in the body, they cause extreme harm, including liver and kidney failure. Did you know? Do you know? Just look at the fine print on the labels or on the internet, and you will see a dandy list of life-threatening conditions promulgated in the use of legally prescribed drugs. It does not have dangerous side effects, on the other hand.

In addition to your regular detoxification system, our naturalist friend Dr. Jacob from Kerala in Southern India recommends "extraordinary" detoxification measures. Such techniques include using a neti pot to clean the nose and sinuses, washing of the face, gargle lemon juice, water enema, fruit quicking, and juice fasting. All this detoxifies the skin more intensively than usual day-to-day washing programs. It is rather curious that when I discuss more' advanced' healing and personal transformation methods, the ideas become ever more basic: food, water, internal hygiene, and breathing. This approach is rather unconventional and penetrates the very foundations of human existence in its most basic ways. This method could even seem diametrically opposed to "advances" in modern medicine, such as super-chemical brews and high-tech laser operations.

Crystal Healing Techniques

Energy and Protection Energy and information are all in the physical world. Energy vibrates at different frequencies, but we can not see it because it vibrates too quickly for us. Since our senses are too slow to vibrate, we obtain only pieces of information that will allow us to perceive the chair on which we are seated, our body, other people...

If you go to a room and feel like' cut the atmosphere by a knife,' this is called negative energy, and if you go to a party, I hope that you'll feel the excitement in the air or good energy.

Similarly, by opening our energy centers in healing, meditation, prayer, visualization, and working with crystals, we draw energy waves (negative and positive) to us. We must, therefore, protect ourselves against negative energy.

Grounding is important to do before you start working with your crystals because it keeps you in contact with your earthly world. Working with crystals will take you to a higher level, and if you haven't grounded before you finish your work, you may experience a floating feeling and become emotional (like the healing curve) as you open up and are sensitive to negativity.

To anchor yourself, take three deep breaths, sit on the floor squarely with your feet, and imagine roots from the base of your feet. They widen down the ground, through the earth and down the center of the earth, to make sure you are fully grounded. Try to lift your foot from the floor to test your grounding. If you find that difficult, you know that you are right.

I ask you, Prayer Lady Universe, to encircle me with the pure white light of your divine being. Remove me from all negative vibrations that will be scattered throughout the universe without harm. Please put me in my own full protection golden bubble.

Visualization Visualize yourself standing in a pink bubble and know that nothing but divine white light and unconditional love can pierce this bubble.

White is the color of God's security, and rose is the color of the unconditional love of heart.

Cleansing and blessing the crystals Several ways to clean up crystals. But not all crystals can be placed in water without damage, so it is important to take care of the way your crystals are cleaned.

All manual cleaning has been performed, while crystals are collected from interactions. You'll have to wash them yourself if your crystals are collected elsewhere.

It is advised that a baby's hairbrush is applied to blow crystals with such a great deal of pollution and dust in the atmosphere. It not only removes dust but also gently stimulates crystal.

Before use, crystals must also be blessed. Once the crystal has been cleaned manually, you need to pray, so the crystal is ready to work with you.

I thank Mother Earth for giving these crystals to the good of humanity. A Dear Blessing Universe. I demand that the crystals be blessed so that they release all harmful energies into the world and do not harm any living thing.

Working with Crystals Follow the basic steps before working with your crystals: 1. Protect yourself and ground 2. Cleanse the crystal and bless it 3. Centre, sit with your eyes shut, and focus a few moments on your breathing.

If you're working on a single crystal, hold the crystal with any point to your fingers in your right hand and ask you to release all negative vibrations without harming anything that lives.

Place the crystal in your left hand with your wrist and ask for your direct assistance. Function with the crystal for at least 10 minutes in each hand.

Explore your crystal. When you acquire a new crystal for the first time, you should spend time exploring it. You will find that your sensitivity to its energy field is developed.

Step 1 See your crystal from various angles, close your eyes, and hold it in both hands, showing your thoughts.

Step 2 Place the crystal in both hands and relax in order to visualize the air that moves through the crystal and to respire gently over the crystal, thus generating heat.

Step 3 Sit calmly with your eyes closed and concentrate on the color of your hands, feel how the crystal feels and feel any sensation or thought that crosses your mind.

Step 4 Lie on your solar plexus and feel how it feels, visualize the crystal color, its shape, and any thoughts you take up again.

Once you notice changes with the crystal on your third eye.

A master/teacher from Usui Reiki and a master/teacher from Karuna ® Reiki with experience in education, coaching, and NLP, helping people with nutrition, jobs, friendships, improvements, and personal development.

I work with those who want their wellbeing to be improved and their ability to develop a healthy, empowered, and positive future. I enjoy helping people to refocus, re-energize, and work holistically towards their goals.

Life Healing Energy With Crystals

Many people have used their pure beauty with gem crystals for years. The bulk of pseudo-scientific alternative therapeutic methods, using rocks and crystals for cure but dating back at least six thousand years, include crystal therapy. For good health and safety, the Romans used crystals as talismans. Romanesque and Greek physicians mixed and heated crystals and safely used them with herbal extracts. Ancient Egyptians believed such rocks could restore their health, and they buried the dead with a quartz crystal, which they felt certain brought life to the beloved. The Chinese used them to promote healing, illumination and desire.

Healers, shamans and priests handle crystals today. I have always been intrigued by rocks and crystals, but it was so long before I was included in a festival of minds, bodies, and spirits, with crystals and their healing power. Because crystals vibrate with the energy of the planet, they will help you balance your body with the energy of the world. You too can now vibrate with these crystals at the highest energy-earth energy! This is the start of the healing. With the use of crystals and adaptation to their power, you remove barriers within yourself that enhance your own natural healing force. Many do not understand, but our bodies are programmed for self-correction and natural healing. When life happens, though, we frequently forget that we stop and care for ourselves so often that our bodies are connected with this process of healing and eventually lead to barriers in our physical and mental bodies.

All life-force blockages cause distress, sorrow and even physical body diseases. This is why I use crystals every day to help my life, address my life's needs right now, to relax and clarify things personally or to encourage love and light in my Reiki practice during chakras healing and clearing. Reiki is the Universal Life Force as an alternative therapeutic tool in its simplest form. The tradition is that we can transform the divine energy of life into an individual pattern, which restores and harmonizes the physical and mental bodies and absorbs and assimilates physical, emotional, and spiritual energies. There is a clearing technique that I am using to remove all obstacles in each chakra and a specific crystal. This makes life's energy clear and keeps mind, body and spirit in their perfectly healthy divine state. When we keep our minds, body and mind in high frequencies of love and healing energy, pain, pain and disease are not allowed to manifest and calm in our physical organisms.

This is just a brief description of Chakra's crystal healing. Each crystal has its own specific healing properties and because of its color, a particular chakra resonates.

Our first chakra, the Root Chakra, mainly discusses and vibrates grounding and can be managed with red, brown and black crystals such as hematite & blue tourmaline. Our second Chakra, the Sacred Chakra, is mainly adaptable to orange, carnelian, amber and orange calcite. The third chakra resounds with the yellow crystals like the yellow citrine and solar plexus, which discusses the digestive system and personal power. The fourth chakra, the chakra of the heart, is a description of the mind, lungs and love. The Heart chakra vibrates with all the white and green crystals like the quartz, jade and green aventurines in a soothing way. The fifth chakra interacts and reflects blue crystals such as Blue Agate, Sodalite and Sapphire. The sixth chakra, the third eye chakra, associated with perception and intelligence, vibrates with violet crystals such as amethyst, iolite and fluorite in the healing stage. The 7th Chakra, the CN or Godly Crown Chakra, best represented white and pure crystals like selenite, transparent quartz, and amethyst.

But I had some phenomenal success stories when I began healing crystals, some of the close-knit and precious in the middle. The first success story is that my husband had to work mango. This is the most unpleasant procedure that many people tell me about. This is certainly a problem with a long period of recovery, because in the past five months he recovered approximately three quarters of his movement in this area without pain. I would wake him up at first, while we were sitting and relaxing and finishing every day. So I took a carnelian ball and used the healing ball very fine. The carnelian ball gave him a lovely heat almost like a thermal stone that moved him to relax and heal the muscles that during the operation had been reduced and tamed.

The second success story is close and dear to me, unlike my daughter. Lupus, an inflammatory disease that affects the tissues and muscles of the body, is my sister Deneen. It's a very painful disease that I hear and see from and physicians use it as a test or error before they find a working treatment. Okay, she's still in her sick time because she doesn't know medicine works to alleviate pain every day. I've healed Reiki several times in the past, which only lightened the pressure to remove the belt, but only when I started crystalline therapy, they provided pain relief. I used several glasses to cleanse her chakra, and I told her to wear a Reiki Ready Hematite necklace a couple of hours a day. It was a couple of weeks, and she had no bad day of pain.

My third success story for a few weeks has been for someone who has degenerative disk disease, lower back pain and neck pain because of a spinal disco. While this disorder may have a genetic cause, it is mainly because of normal wear and tear and injury. In this type of illness, baseline pain is usually continuous, often mild. It also involves moderate to severe pain attacks on the back or neck that could usually last a few days and may get worse before the person returns to the pain department as normal. Rachael had degenerative disk disease when she came to me for many years. I supported her with Reiki's soothing power and a carnelian ball I solved with lower back problems. I used Hematite on her after both these things, which, for her, was just like Belle of a Ball. As hematite stones came into contact with the skin in the lower back, she almost immediately reported the pain dissolution and laid on her back until Hematite stopped. I advised her to begin this treatment alone while she was not with me and to clean hepatitis with a selenite stone to take away all the negative elements and toxins before returning to her home.

Although many of our ancestors have recorded the use of healing crystals, some still question the use of these stones and other types of alternative medicine. No numerous studies can demonstrate medicine as a cure for mind, body and spirit, such as reiki, acupuncture, crystal healing, and even yoga. That doesn't mean that these healing processes don't work. This means only that money is not spent on new age medicine, the same natural remedy as it was once healed. Despite a lack of studies of this type of treatment, approximately one third of Americans still use alternative medicines. Crystal therapy is not a cure for everyone. You should still seek the assistance and care of your doctor, but as you can see from three very different conditions, all healing efforts are enhanced by the crystal curative stone. Whether you have emotional wounds, physical conditions, or just need the power to be enhanced, crystals vibrate the same way.

CONCLUSION

A chakra relates to the life-force power and transmits it; it is the equilibrium point within the body. Charka comes from the Sanskrit word, which describes a wheel or a sound energy sphere that is continuously spinning.

Some conventional Hindu scriptures say that a person's body has approximately 90,000 points of Chakra. However, seven Chakras are more critical than the rest. Such chakras live from the base of the spine to the top of the head.

The base or root chakras are the origins of these chakras. Then we move up the column with the Chakra of the sex or the navel, with the plexus of the stomach or the solar plexus, the Chakra of the heart, the Chakra of the throat, the Chakra of the brow or the third eye and the Chakra. Such seven significant chakras receive and transmit signals from the natural universe or the infinite cosmos. It affects an individual's religious, metaphysical, mental, cognitive, bodily, and psychological status.

Chakras have been defined in various ways, but they all have one common feature. Whether from Chinese medicine or the Hindu perspective, all these explanations are identical. It is the perception of people's experiences and the way that the human mind thinks and feels different emotions.

Whether we are awake or not, the chakras are in constant movement. The structure, behavior, physical conditions, glandular processes, and our thoughts and actions will affect this continuous activity. Nevertheless, if there is a chakra malfunction in one or more points that may be triggered by different reasons, a disequilibrium may evolve and become evident in other areas of our being.

It is believed that the chakras are associated with the endocrine joy in our bodies. If a chakra gets out of balance, then we can have so-called trouble in the normal behavior of the endocrine gland and everything connected or connected to that gland.

You can say that any significant illnesses or diseases that may affect your body can be associated with an unbalanced chakra. It is essential to maintain the correct balance of chakras to ensure that your body works correctly. While you may not see the physical characteristics of a disease or imbalance, you may see a difference in your emotions.

The repressed and overlooked emotional baggage we bear because of those traumatic experiences is one of the significant causes of a chakra imbalance. Most people usually enjoy their bad memories without realizing that these psychological toxins that are hidden inside them affect their cellular bodies.

Thus it is necessary once and for all to deal with emotional baggage to maintain a proper balance of the chakras, which initiates a healing process in order, to begin with, the physical self.

You should know that chakra healing is perfect for your body and that you can affect every one of your chakras directly. You can do so using methods such as Reiki treatment, color therapy, aromatherapy, pendulum chakra balance, crystals, or gemstones.

Many people like to do yoga classes that help with their breathing and physical exercises. Yoga is good to keep chakra balance in the body, as it allows people to concentrate.

Many approaches to treat chakras include meditation and guided visualization. This is often done through relaxing music CDs that help to promote natural healing by relaxing techniques. It helps reduce pressure and harness our mind's energy.

Even when we know that we can't touch or see our Chakra, we can help each other to make the best of our bodies.

The human body needs to be healthy and properly fed so that we can have a balanced chakra. Foods help to maintain the balance of each of the seven primary chakras.

Root vegetables and foods rich in protein and spices help feed the root chakra. The holy Chakra that blends sex and imagination is nurtured by things such as sweet fruit, nuts, cinnamon, coffee, and seeds such as sesame and cabbage. The solar plexus chakra feeds spicy mintstones, dairy products, yogurt, pasta, bread, and cereals that inspire our sense of self-reliance and self-love.

Are you aware that the heart chakra best works on leafy vegetables and even many green tea types? The Chakra of the throat always needs a lot of hydrating fluids. Water and even fruit juices like apple and orange juice are the most active liquids.

The 3rd eye chakra thrives on strawberries, blueberries, and wine.

The crown chakra needs proper detoxification in our emotional and spiritual center. This is achieved by ceremonial inhalation of spices, fasts, and incense.

We are always safe by trying to keep our chakras balanced. It makes us more in tune with our surroundings and allows others to live in the spiritual world in which we live.

www.ingramcontent.com/pod-product-compliance
Lightning Source LLC
Chambersburg PA
CBHW070846250726
48662CB00003B/1381